TEACHING CHILDREN THE BIBLE

Teaching Children the Bible

New Models in Christian Education

Marion Pardy

1817

HARPER & ROW, PUBLISHERS, SAN FRANCISCO

Cambridge, Hagerstown, New York, Philadelphia, Washington
London, Mexico City, São Paulo, Singapore, Sydney

FIRST EDITION

Library of Congress Cataloging-in-Publication DATA

Pardy, Marion.
    Teaching children the Bible.

    Bibliography: p.
    Includes index.
    1. Bible—Evidences, authority, etc.
2. Christian education of children.
3. Piaget, Jean, 1896–1980
I. title.
BS480.P27   1988   220′.07   87-45193
ISBN 0-06-254829-8 (pbk.)

88 89 90 91 92 MPC 10 9 8 7 6 5 4 3 2 1

Contents

Acknowledgements

Many lives have touched mine in the production of this thesis. All merit recognition; however, space is limited to major contributors. I, therefore, acknowledge the following:

Pamela Verrill Walker, who gave me the courage and confidence to resume academic study;

Barrie Wilson, whose gift of critical examination motivated, challenged, prodded, and supported me in the whole process;

Barrie Wilson, Bill Coleman, and Stewart Crysdale, my supervisory committee, who provided time and expertise in reading, critiquing, and encouraging;

Glenys Lee, for her painstaking care in typing and personal interest in the midst of a busy schedule;

The faculty of graduate studies, York University, for their financial support and flexibility, enabling me to pursue a research area of interest;

The United Church of Canada, for its continuing education program, providing time and financial assistance to complete this thesis.

Finally, I thank all of those unnamed friends whose expressions of interest and words of encouragement kept the spirit high and the motivation continuous.

Illustrations

Introduction

This book is primarily concerned with the nature and authority of the Bible for Christians. That is, by what criterion or criteria can Christians claim authoritative uniqueness for the Bible?

Findings indicate that most research omits or inadequately resolves this question. This concern is of paramount importance to Christian educators, for in their ministry of teaching biblical heritage (a primary task of all Christian churches) and training others to teach it, both content and methodology are strongly affected by one's understanding of the nature and authority of the Bible. Much is written on the role of the Bible, biblical methodology, and so forth—all based on the unexamined premise of biblical authority. Explicit and implicit hypotheses such as "The Bible is the Word of God" and "The Bible is the only infallible rule of faith," which demand critical examination, are unattested. Other authors raise the question of authority sufficiently to discover a relationship between biblical authority and canon but neglect the essential continuing research. What are the implications of claiming the compatibility of biblical authority and canon? One logical response to this question is the ecclesiological position of Roman Catholicism—an "infallible" Bible must have an "infallible" church in matters of biblical interpretation. Most Protestant churches, knowing too well how church decisions are made, are more than hesitant to adopt this stance as part of their doctrinal proclamation! The validity of this position is more seriously challenged through such writings as *The Gnostic Gospels* in which the author illuminates the process of canonization through an exploration and examination of a pivotal event inaugurating canonical activity, namely, the political challenge to established orthodox Christianity by other significant Christian voices (for example, the Gnostics).

Within the acquiescence to biblical authority shared by Christendom are differing views concerning the nature and depth of this authority. Indeed, differing views are identified within individual denominations as illustrated in this paper through a critical examination of biblical authority in The United Church of Canada. Here three existing views or models are portrayed.

Through the process of presentation and critical examination of materials concerning the nature and authority of Scripture, of child development, and of Christian education, the end result of this study proffers an alternative model for biblical education with children.

Part I examines the nature and authority of the Bible as portrayed first in The United Church of Canada and then in two representative thinkers in hermeneutics, Johann August Ernesti (1707–81) from the post-Reformation era and Hans-Georg Gadamer (1900–), a contemporary philosopher. The following paragraphs outline the route and rationale of this examination and derived conclusions.

Chapters 1 and 2 are a survey and critical examination of the official positions concerning biblical authority in The United Church of Canada through an exploration of its doctrinal and educational materials. There are several reasons for this choice of denomination. First of all, The United Church of Canada is the largest Protestant denomination in Canada. Through the union of the Methodist, Congregational, and Presbyterian Churches (approximately one quarter of the Presbyterians chose not to join) The United Church of Canada came into being in 1925. With unity as a continuing goal, the Evangelical United Brethren joined the union in 1968. With unity also came the necessity of diversity; that is, to accommodate differences as well as commonalities. Second, publicly it proclaims a liberal, learned approach to theology and education. Third, it is also the chosen church of my membership and profession. The outcome of this study portrays three operative models of biblical authority, as previously indicated, each with its own inadequacies and each incompatible with the others.

Chapter 3 is a presentation and critical examination of Johann August Ernesti concerning biblical authority and interpretation. I chose Ernesti for two major reasons. He is representative of classical scholarship and Protestant biblical hermeneutics, yet largely unknown to the North American audience. In *The Historical-Critical Method* he is acclaimed by Edgar Krentz as the "father of the profane scientific interpretation of the Bible."[1] Second, Ernesti serves as a "middle-person" between extreme radicalism and pietism since he also "denied the possibility of inspired scripture ever erring."[2] The *Oxford Dictionary of the Christian Church* acclaims the chief importance of Ernesti as offering "an attempt to reconcile the theological position of his church with historical criticism of the Bible, in opposition alike to uncritical rationalism and to mystical and allegorical interpretation."[3] Ernesti demonstrates how historically the Protestant church addressed the problem of biblical authority, identifying the difficulties of using undebatable premises such as the inerrancy of Scripture. Nevertheless, his contribution to the field of general hermeneutics is noteworthy and aids this discussion through its scholarly emphases and through illuminating the problem.

Chapter 4 presents and examines the hermeneutic of Hans-Georg Gadamer. Gadamer was chosen as representative of a contemporary philosophical position that has influenced numerous other contemporary writings in the study of interpretation.

Part I concludes with examining the implications for biblical understanding of Gadamer's hermeneutic. As a result of this examination, the claim is made that the essential ingredients of his hermeneutic are consistent with biblical thought, thus demonstrating the usefulness of Gadamer's hermeneutic in determining the nature of biblical authority.

The additional concern of this book, explored in Part II, is the Christian education of children concerning the Bible, noting that a primary task of all Christian churches is to introduce the biblical heritage to children. While mainline (Roman Catholic, United Church of Canada, Anglican, Presbyterian, Lutheran) and fundamentalist churches disagree on approach and content, all share this common task and endow the Bible with unique authority. It is imperative to explore this area of Christian education, for the content and methodology of teaching the Bible are strongly influenced by an understanding of the nature and authority of Scripture underlying the teaching.

The route for exploring this concern is a presentation of the influential model of developmental psychology concerning children espoused by Jean Piaget (1896–1980).

Piaget's works are classic in the field of child development theory and any research concerning children and education is inadequate without comprehensive knowledge of this work. Having critically examined Piaget from a nonfundamentalist perspective, this book then moves on to consider implications of Piagetian theory for Christian education.

On the basis of the theological, philosophical, and educational findings of the above, the analysis and conclusion of the whole book, in Part III, proposes an alternative biblical model for Christian education with children in The United Church of Canada and kindred denominations. It is demonstrated that this model is congruent with the authority of Scripture; with a critical biblical and theological stance; with child development and educational theory.

One further explanatory note is required. Language shapes and informs thought. Inclusive language (nonsexist word usage in relation to humanity and divinity) is the proclivity of this text; where direct quotes are cited, however, no editorial changes have been made.

It is hoped that the questions evoked will motivate inquirers to continuous research towards further legitimate models of biblical authority and education.

I. THE NATURE AND AUTHORITY OF THE BIBLE

1. Three Models of Biblical Authority

The professed doctrine of a church is an obvious place of research for examining the nature and authority of Scripture. Doctrinal views concerning Scripture are also manifested in practice, that is, in views held on social and global issues, in worship, and in materials set forth for the education of the people. Chapters 1 and 2 explore the question "What does The United Church of Canada say concerning the nature and authority of Scripture?" through an examination of official doctrinal statements and through the curricula recommended by the United Church. Because in its formation in 1925 the United Church represented three major Protestant denominations of Methodism, Presbyterianism, and Congregationalism, many Protestant denominations can locate their position within one or more of the biblical stances portrayed through the United Church's doctrinal and educational statements. The process demonstrated in this book is also transferable to all other denominations; readers may use the model of examining the official statements of their own denomination in order to ascertain the nature and authority of Scripture in their own church.

Official Church Documents

The foundational basis of all three models (the ultimate authority model, the contextual model, and the christocentric model) can be found in official doctrinal statements of The United Church of Canada: "Basis of Union," 1925; *A Statement of Faith,* 1940; "Confessing our Faith" report, 1982.

Basis of Union—Ultimate Authority Model

Those arguing for ultimate authority of Scripture can legitimately refer to the "Basis of Union," the official document of doctrine and polity giving birth to The United Church of Canada in 1925. The "Basis of Union" is the basic law of the church and can be changed only by action of General Council, the highest decision-making court of the church, after a majority vote by pastoral charges and/or presbyteries.

The format of the "Basis of Union" is an introduction followed by twenty articles or paragraphs pertaining to church doctrine. A sampling of article headings includes "Of God," "Of Revelation," "Of the Sin of Man," "Of the Lord Jesus Christ," and "Of Prayer." Noticeably absent is an article "Of Scripture." References to Scripture are contained, however, in the content of the document. The introduction states as follows:

We affirm our belief in the Scriptures of the Old and New Testaments as the primary source and ultimate standard of Christian faith and life.[1]

The articles are then introduced as "a brief summary of our common faith . . . in substance agreeable to the teaching of the Holy Scriptures."[2]

Two further references to Scripture are contained in the articles:

Article II. Of Revelation

We receive the Holy Scriptures of the Old and New Testaments, given by the inspiration of God, as containing the only infallible rule of faith and life, a faithful record of God's gracious revelations, and as the sure witness of Christ.[3]

Article XIV. Of the Law of God

We believe that the moral law of God, summarized in the Ten Commandments, testified to by the prophets and unfolded in the life and teachings of Jesus Christ, stands forever in truth and equity, and is not made void by faith, but on the contrary is established thereby.[4]

Any concern for the lack of prominence given to Scripture as an article heading is alleviated by the magnitude of authority ascribed to it in key words and phrases contained above: "primary," "ultimate," "only infallible rule," "stands forever in truth and equity."

Summary points of the ultimate authority of the Bible, according to the "Basis of Union," are as follows:

1. Scripture is the primary source and ultimate standard of Christian faith and life,
2. Scripture is given through inspiration by God;
3. Scripture contains (a) the only infallible rule of faith and life, (b) a faithful record of God's gracious revelations, and (c) sure witness of Christ.
4. The Ten Commandments . . . stand forever in truth and equity. This biblical stance is pictured in illustration 1.

Confessing Our Faith—Contextual Model

The current trend in the United Church is directed away from doctrinal statements written by the "theological experts." At the twenty-ninth meeting of the General Council in Montreal, 1982, the Theology and Faith Committee proposed a process, for approval by Council, whereby church members and adherents through the var-

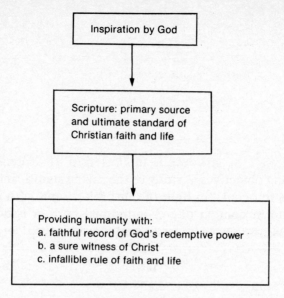

1. Ultimate Authority Model

ious committees and courts of the church "explore our heritage, clarify our beliefs, and experience the joy of new faith commitments."[5] In an introduction entitled "A Believing People in a Changing World," the following commentary is made:

When asked "What does the United Church believe?" we, as members of the United Church, point to the Basis of Union, to the 1940 Statement of Faith, and primarily to works of faith. This denomination does witness through its work and through its engagement with issues. For some time now, these ways have been sufficient.

But the situation has changed. Earlier statements on life and faith do not speak to or for many in the church, or outside it. Our struggle to be faithful to God's love for a broken world takes place in a radically different context.[6]

The proposed process will spread over approximately ten years, after which the General Council will make a decision as to "how our church may confess our faith for its time."[7] Three themes comprise the process:

- The saving significance of Jesus,
- The nature and purpose of God,
- The meaning and mission of the church

Reference to Scripture is identified in the statements outlining objectives. A study of the saving significance of Jesus is to occur "in light of our biblical and faith heritage and in context of . . . individual current issues."[8] Likewise, the resources produced to enable implementation of this theme are to "take into account the biblical witness, our confessional heritage, ecumenical and global contexts in format appropriate to their designated constituencies, e.g. taking into account age, background and experience of constituents."[9]

The development places biblical authority in the context of a global and contextual theology. Principal claims of this model are as follows:

1. God is revealed through tradition, Scripture, various expressions of faith, the world, and current personal and societal issues,
2. The focus of God's love is the world,
3. Scripture is one resource for theological understanding and for discerning what it means to be "faithful to God's love for a broken world."

Statement of Faith: A Catechism—Christocentric Model

The Christocentric model finds expression in two other official documents of The United Church of Canada (official in that they were approved by the General

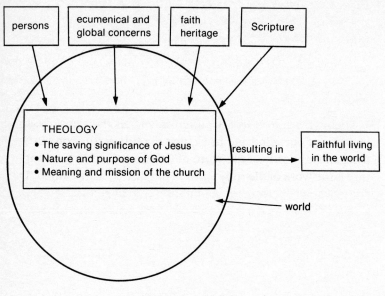

2. Contextual Model

Council of the church): *Statement of Faith* (authorized by the ninth General Council—1940) and *A Catechism* (authorized by the tenth General Council—1942), a catechetical simplification of *Statement of Faith*. Unlike the "Basis of Union," *Statement of Faith* contains an identifiable section, "The Holy Scriptures" (section IV):

We believe that the great moments of God's revelation and communication of Himself to men are recorded and interpreted in the Scriptures of the Old and New Testament.

We believe that, while God uttered His Word to man in many portions progressively, the whole is sufficient to declare His mind and will for our salvation. To Israel He made Himself known as a holy and righteous God and a Saviour; the fulness of truth and grace came by Jesus Christ. The writings were collected and preserved by the Church.

We believe that the theme of all Holy Scripture is the redemptive purpose and working of God, and that herein lies its unity.

We believe that in Holy Scripture God claims the complete allegiance of our mind and heart; that the full persuasion of the truth and authority of the Word of God contained in the Scripture is the work of the Holy Spirit in our hearts; that, using Holy Scripture, the Spirit takes the things of Christ and shows them unto us for our spiritual nourishment and growth in grace.

So we acknowledge in Holy Scripture the true witness to God's Word and the sure guide to Christian faith and conduct.[10]

References to the Bible in *A Catechism* are contained in the following questions and answers:

30. What is the Bible?

The Bible is the record of God's increasing revelation of himself to his ancient people Israel and to the early Church; it is Christ that gives meaning to the whole revelation.

31. What is the chief purpose of the Bible?

The chief purpose of the Bible is to tell us what God has done to save us from sin and evil, and to claim for him the complete allegiance of mind and will.

51. How are we to read the Bible?

We are to listen for the Word of God contained in the Bible with attention and desire, lay it upon our hearts, and practice it in our lives.

52. What benefits flow from reading the Bible?

If we receive God's word humbly and thankfully, we shall come to know his mind and accept his will, and we shall receive strength to do what he requires of us.[11]

In contrast to the "Basis of Union," the absoluteness of the authority of Scripture is significantly reduced. Phrases like "ultimate standard," "only infallible rule," and "stands forever in truth and equity" are now replaced by phrases of "true witness" and "sure guide." The historical and theological nature of the Bible and the concept of progressive revelation are also granted greater prominence.

Key concepts in the biblical understanding of these statements are:

1. Scripture records and interprets the great moments of God's revelation and communication of God to humankind.
2. The theme and unity of Scripture is the redemptive purpose and working of God.
3. Through the work of the Holy Spirit, we grasp the truth and authority of the Word, are nourished spiritually, and grow in grace.
4. Scripture is the true witness to God's Word and the sure guide to Christian faith and conduct.
5. Christ gives meaning to the whole revelation contained in Scripture.

Accordingly, this model is pictured in illustration 3.

The Founding Denominations

A study of the biblical stances of the Presbyterian, Congregational, and Methodist churches, the founding members of The United Church of Canada in 1925, fur-

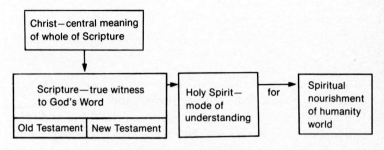

3. Christocentric Model

ther demonstrates that each denomination's understanding of Scripture is compatible with one of the three models described above. A study of these individual churches supports the thesis that the Presbyterian church professed primarily the ultimate authority model, the Congregational church the contextual model, and the Methodist church bore the seeds of the Christocentric model.[12]

Ultimate Authority Model—Presbyterian Church

The ultimate authority model of Scripture is observed in *The Confession of Faith* of the Presbyterian church. In chapter 1, "Of Holy Scripture," containing ten articles or sections, the following key claims are identified:

III. The Books commonly called Apocrypha not being of divine inspiration, are no part of the canon of scripture; and therefore are of no authority in the Church of God, nor to be any otherwise approved, or made use of, than other human writings.

IV. The authority of the holy scripture, for which it ought to be believed and obeyed, dependeth not upon the testimony of any man or church, but wholly upon God (who is truth itself) the author thereof; and therefore it is to be received, because it is the word of God.

VII. All things in scripture, are not alike plain in themselves, nor alike clear unto all; yet those things which are necessary to be known, believed, and observed, for salvation, are so clearly propounded and opened in some places of Scripture or other, that not only the learned, but the unlearned, in a due sense of the ordinary means, may attain unto a sufficient understanding of them.

IX. The infallible rule of interpretation of Scripture, is, the scripture itself; and, therefore, when there is a question about the true and full sense of any scripture, (which is not manifold, but one) it must be searched and known by other places that speak more clearly.

X. The supreme Judge, by which all controversies of religion are to be determined and all decrees of councils, opinions of ancient writers, doctrines of men, and private spirits, are to be examined, and in whose sentence we are to rest, can be no other but the Holy Spirit, speaking in the scripture.[13]

To further the biblical cause, three questions were asked of ministers at their ordination:

Do you believe the Scriptures of the Old and New Testaments to be the Word of God, and the only rule of faith and manners?

Do you sincerely own and believe the whole doctrine contained in the Confession of Faith, approved by the General Assemblies of this Church, and ratified by law in the year 1690, to be founded upon the Word of God, . . . ?

Are you persuaded that the Presbyterian government and discipline of this Church are founded upon the Word of God . . . ?[14]

This biblical passion permeated Presbyterianism. In the *History of the Presbyterian Church in the Dominion of Canada,* William Gregg summarized the position:

In common with other Evangelical Christians, Presbyterians acknowledge the sixty-six canonical books of the Old and New Testament Scriptures as the sole, supreme, authoritative rule of faith and life. They reject the authority of the Apocryphal books, and of the traditions of men, oral and written.

As to the Worship of God, Presbyterians maintain the general principle that nothing is to be required or admitted into religious observances which is not either explicitly or implicitly sanctioned by the Word of God. They object not merely to everything in the substance and modes of worship which is contrary to the teachings of Scripture, but to everything for which a warrant cannot be found in the inspired volume.[15]

So entrenched was Presbyterianism in this position of ultimate authority, that the dissenters from church union based their argument on Scripture, claiming that many features of the "Basis of Union" were "inconsistent with the Standards of the Church," which is founded upon Scripture.[16] Within the Presbyterian church, the advocates for church union argued that the "Basis of Union" did not contain "features inconsistent with the Scriptures."[17]

Contextual Model—Congregational Church

The Congregationalists, too, claimed Scripture as the authoritative foundation for doctrine and polity, but in the context of the democratic spirit of congregational autonomy. Their legacy to The United Church of Canada

was a nonfundamentalist approach to Scripture. Historically, the Congregationalists "insisted on the production
of definite authority from the Holy Scriptures in support
of every detail of Church organization and of every
church rule and practice"[18] as a corrective to the abusive
practices observed in the church. This entrenchment
changed to an awareness of the church not imprisoned by
the "letter of the law" to one freed by the Spirit. Scripture still claimed authority, but Scripture was recognized
as having an historical and cultural context.[19]

The basic principle of Congregationalism became,
thus, "the supreme leadership of Christ and the priest-
hood of all believers; the autonomy of the local church;
and the fellowship both of Christian brethren within the
Church and of the churches with another."[20]

The statement of doctrine of the Congregational
church contains the traditional belief statement of
Scripture:

We believe the Scriptures of the Old and New Testaments are
the record of God's revelation of Himself in the work of redemption; that they were written by men under special guid-
ance of the Holy Spirit; that they are able to make wise unto
salvation; and that they constitute an authoritative standard by
which religious teaching and human conduct are to be regu-
lated and judged.[21]

Clarification of this doctrine demonstrates a nonfundamentalist stance. The following questions and answers
are contained in *A Manual for Christian Instruction:*

7. Have we a record of God's redemptive revelation to man?

We have. The Bible, including the Old and New Testaments, is a partial record of that revelation. Some of
God's revelations were not recorded, and some that were

recorded have been lost. The Bible, however, is a record of those great spiritual truths, a knowledge of which is essential to man's salvation and happiness.

10. Are all the books of the Bible of equal importance?

The books of the Bible are not all of equal importance. They all are necessary; but, like the members of the human body, some are more excellent than others . . . Isaiah is a sublimer revelation than Leviticus. John's Gospel surpasses the Epistle of James. Proverbs and Ecclesiastes contain practical suggestions relative to the conduct of life; but they do not sound the depths of the religious nature as do the Psalms, nor do they bear witness to the historic work of Christ, or to man's great Helper, the Holy Spirit. . . .

12. What is the relation of the record of revelation to the teachings of revelation?

The literary form and characteristics of the books of the Bible are important; and attention must be given to them if we would grasp the living truth of which they are the vehicle. . . . It is, however, true that words are but the clothes which the Scriptural teachings wear. . . . Disproportionate emphasis on the letter of garment of the living Word of God, be it in the interest of conservatism or radicalism, is scribism pure and simple.[22]

All doctrinal statements and amplifications within Congregationalism must be read in the context of autonomous congregational polity.

Its government is vested in the body of believers who compose it. It is subject to the control of no other ecclesiastical body, but it recognizes and sustains the obligations of mutual counsel and cooperation which are common among Congre-

gational churches, and it is in fellowship with all churches
which acknowledge Jesus the Christ to be their divine Re-
deemer and Lord.[23]

The Contextual model discussed above in the "Confessing Our Faith" document is primarily a contemporary
expression of the biblical base of Congregationalism.

Christocentric Model—Methodist Church

The doctrine of the Methodist church claims Scripture
as the only sufficient resource for salvation:

The Holy Scriptures contain all things necessary to salvation;
so that whatsoever is not read therein, nor may be proved
thereby, is not to be required of any man that it should be believed as an article of faith, or be thought requisite or necessary to salvation. . . .[24]

Further to this, the reason that the authority of the Old
Testament is posed as unproblematic is that Christ is central to both Testaments.[25]

This position on the authority of Scripture is under-
scored by the question asked of those being received into
full membership in the church:

Question:
Do you believe in the inspiration and divine authority of the
Holy Scriptures, and accept the same as a sufficient rule of
faith and practice?

Answer:
I do.[26]

A similar question is asked of those being ordained:

Question:
Are you persuaded that the Holy Scriptures contain sufficiently all doctrines required of necessity for eternal salvation

through faith in Jesus Christ. And are you determined out of the said Scriptures to instruct the people committed to your charge, and to teach nothing as required of necessity to eternal salvation, but that which you shall be persuaded may be concluded and proved by the Scriptures?

Answer:
I am so persuaded, and have so determined, by God's grace.[27]

This *sola scriptura* stance is compatible with the Protestant reformers and with John Wesley himself, "not in the sense that tradition and experience have no value, but in the sense that these further sources of insight must be congruous with the revelation recorded in Scripture."[28]

Reference to the centrality of Christ as justification of the Old Testament shows the centrality of Christ to be the unifying force of Scripture and the reason for the exaltation of Scripture.

Concerning Scripture and Opposition to Church Union

Some would query why some Presbyterians opposed church union if the biblical undergirding was congruent with their own doctrine and why the Methodists and Congregationalists supported it without major public dissent. The following factors are offered in response:

1. The impetus for church union was economical and geographical, not theological,
2. Some Presbyterians were entrenched in Presbyterianism, and many polity features of the "Basis of Union" were "inconsistent with the standards of the Church," which they claimed was founded upon Scriptures.[29]
3. Key leadership positions in all three churches were held by conservatives.[30]

4. The Joint Committee for Church Union was comprised of older ministers. "For the most part they were men whose mentality was, to say the least, fully matured, and from whom no radical departure would probably be expected."[31]

The mode for dealing with the scriptural controversy at the time (that is, the rationalistic interpretation of Scripture proffered among some professors in theological colleges and some leading Congregational ministers) was essentially avoidance because, as identified above, doctrinal concerns were secondary.

In the United Church story the unresolved controversy concerning the authority and applicability of Scripture continues as identified in the three models illustrated above. It is imperative that the authority of Scripture be seen as a primary rather than secondary concern, as the church's response to issues confronting our world and church today is greatly influenced by doctrinal understanding. Arguments supporting or opposing paramount issues such as homosexuality, role and place of women, inclusive language, abortion, nuclear disarmament, civil disobedience, poverty, etc. resort to Scripture for ammunition. In its educational program, controversy over the content and methodology of curriculum resources is also scripturally oriented.

Having identified three models of Scripture in the official doctrinal statements of the United Church influenced by the founding denominations, let us now examine the curricula recommended by the United Church in light of these models to view how doctrine manifests itself in practice.

2. Biblical Authority and Curricula

The Ministry with Children Working Unit presently recommends to its constituency the choice of four curricula
of varying educational approaches. Because of its diversity within unity (amalgamation of four denominations and
the variety within each) the choice and production of
one curriculum is problematic within The United
Church of Canada. A pluralistic approach offering
choices of curricula seemed more feasible. Nationally
this task of choosing and recommending curricula resides
with the Ministry with Children Working Unit, a committee of the Division of Mission in Canada responsible for
all aspects of the church's ministry with children (worship, education, pastoral care, decision making, social
and justice issues, and so forth). It then recommends its
findings to the constituency. Congregations are encouraged to choose one or more depending upon their understanding of Christian education and the particular needs
of their congregation. The four curricula deemed compatible with the Working Unit's theological and educational stance (see the Appendix) are as follows, though
these are subject to change because of changes in curricula availability, content changes, and the *Future Directions* Project of the United Church:

- *Core* curriculum, formerly called *The New Curriculum,* was initially published by The United Church of
  Canada in 1964. Adult education was prized as a prerequisite for those who teach children and youth. Ex

tensive background was provided for teachers pertaining to theological understanding, child development, and pedagogy. Students' books dealt with historical content of Scripture and church. Through its three-year thematic cycle of "God and His Purpose," "Jesus Christ and the Christian Life," and "The Church in the World," this curriculum provided the opportunity for a sound theological education for children and adults in peer groupings.

- *Loaves and Fishes,* another United Church publication, was initially published in 1978, in response to the need for materials responding to the pastoral concerns of children. That is, the curriculum attempts to begin with the faith/life questions of children and bring to those questions the resources of the Christian faith: Scripture, church history, worship, prayer, contemporary stories, etc. The resource is "grass roots" in that individual units are developed and tested in local congregations, with selection and editorial work (including biblical and theological background) written nationally. Two volumes are produced annually, and considerable time for leader preparation is demanded.

- *Joy,* a curriculum initially published in 1972 and fully revised in 1986 by Winston Press (United States), focuses on the need for children to know, experientially and cognitively, what it means to belong to Christian community. Materials from nursery to grade 6 for children and teachers are graded according to the capabilities of children based on Piaget's theory of child development. The curriculum is classified as child-centered in that the primary focus is on the needs of children, rather than content.

- *Children's Bible Series* is published jointly by eight denominations in the United States of America and supported by the Presbyterian Church in Canada, the Baptist Federation of Canada, and the United Church of Canada (the United Church's involvement is in the purchase and recommendation of materials). The primary concern of this curriculum is to teach biblical stories to children in a comprehensive way. Materials from nursery to junior (9–11 years) are graded departmentally (that is 3–5 years; 6–8 years; 9–11 years) and are produced quarterly.

The Working Unit developed its own theological and educational stance as a canon or measurement tool to assess the suitability of curriculum and other resources. An examination and critique of this document, together with the recommended curricula, will highlight the three previously described concepts of biblical authority.

Theological and Educational Stance, 1982 (Revised 1986)

Biblical themes and images permeate this document (which is reprinted in the Appendix) with key primary images being the "Body of Christ" and "Shalom." These images stress the belief of belonging in the church (children and adults) and the mandate for love, peace, and justice. Jesus is pivotal to the faith with belief in him as essential for Christians.

Jesus Christ is the person through whom Christians believe they receive salvation—are made whole—at one with God. . . .[1]

This exclusiveness of Jesus for Christians is significant, for elsewhere other faiths merit recognition. In Christian education with children a key concept is that "God loves and cares for everyone and for all of God's creation."[2] To be faithful to this faith statement, programs for children in the church need to "convey in appropriate forms that we respect other people's sacred literature and leaders so that we can respect others as people of faith."[3]

In a cultural context where children will undoubtedly meet people with differing belief systems, Christians are challenged to know their story and, at the same time, view themselves as part of the whole of humanity:

As members of the entire human family, the Judaeo-Christian community, the United Church community and a local congregation, we acknowledge there are times when we feel bereft and hopeless. As Christians, we believe we have a faith/story which offers us a sense of belonging, hope and a base from which to live in our world.[4]

The Bible's importance is observed in two primary ways. As indicated above, the biblical images and themes are authoritative for faith statements. This is evident in statements pertaining to Jesus' attitude to children, reference to Paul, declarations about Jesus' teachings, etc.[5] It is assumed that these biblical references substantiate faith statements. The Bible's significance is also evidenced in the fact that part of the Christians' story is contained therein. Two biblical mandates follow in the midst of other mandates:

- "Tell each other the biblical story of the people of God. . . ."
- "Discover the context in which the Bible was written and relate it to individual and corporate life today."[6]

These biblical mandates are not the whole story, however. In addition to the biblical story there are "stories of our Christian tradition, our denominational heritage, and our congregational history."[7] Part of the story is also "the basic doctrines of our faith," participants' own personal stories, and the stories enacted through the worshipping community.[8] In programs with children it is recommended that their worldview, questions, and concerns be the starting point of methodology and that an approach that combines education, action, and worship be used.[9] The *raison d'etre* of knowing and sharing these stories is "action faith" expressed in the world today:

We are called to act so that God's love can be shared with the world through us; so that we and the world can live as God intended.[10]

Of paramount significance also is the claim that Scripture does not provide the whole of understanding of the nature of God. The claim is that "God is beyond our comprehension." We look to insights we have received through Scripture, Jesus Christ, personal and community experiences.

In summary, then, ingredients to discern God's will today are the world, the tradition, the church, persons, and the Bible. Obviously, this theological and educational stance relates primarily to the contextual model of the previous chapter.

Core Curriculum

The *Core* curriculum is described by Dr. Peter Gordon White, former Deputy Secretary for theology and faith in The United Church of Canada, as the "most official body of teaching the United Church has ever had." The presuppositions were voted on and approved by the eighteenth General Council in 1958. Here the scholars of the church attempted to write for the laity of the church. The *Core* curriculum is a collection of approximately thirty-three books: a three-year repeatable cycle of students' books and teachers' guides from primary (beginning at age 6) to adult, one year for nursery, and a two-year cycle for kindergarten. For this comparison I have chosen the *Prospectus,* the *Junior Teacher's Guide* (year 1) and the introductory adult study book, *The Word and the Way.*

The Prospectus

Here the purpose of Christian education is defined as follows: "that persons at each stage of their lives may know God as he is revealed in Jesus Christ, serving him in love through the worship and work fellowship and witness of the church."[11] This purpose proclaims a basic creedal conviction of the Christian faith (namely, God's revelation in Jesus Christ) acknowledges that knowledge of God is apprehended differently according to a person's development ("at each stage"), and suggests that such knowledge results in loving service.

God's revelation in Jesus Christ is declared as the central theme of the gospel:

The Christian gospel is the saving message from God with your name on it. It is a personal message. . . . It may come to you in the words of Scripture. It comes with real power in God's living word, our Lord Jesus Christ. The gospel is the proclamation of what God has done. Its central theme is the life, death, and resurrection of Jesus.[12]

The whole Bible has the unifying theme of "the redemptive purpose and work of God." It is described as having "a unique place" in Christian education to be read "seriously but not literalistically." Again, the primary significant moments in Scripture are those related to Jesus Christ.

It (the Bible) confronts with the Word of God those who come to it in faith, especially where it presents Jesus Christ, the Word become flesh.[13]

The Statement of Faith declaration of the Bible as "a sure guide to Christian faith and conduct" is upheld.

The authority of Scripture rests in the assumption that "Scripture is the written record of revelation, God's disclosure of himself to man." And because persons today are part of human history, Scripture "can become a revelation of God's dealings with us in this time and place." To be noted here is the concept of a continuum history. The purpose of biblical study, then, is to "prepare the way for people to perceive God and to respond to Him in the present in a continuing encounter."[14] To accomplish this task, a historical-critical approach to Scripture is highlighted as a necessary, though not simple, task.[15]

In relation to children, biblical usage takes differing forms (from contagion to content) depending upon their stage of development.

At times portions may be brought to bear on discernible needs of particular age groups. But always the Bible must be allowed to make its own impact on the reader. . . . For this reason, it is desirable, at appropriate age levels, for persons to come to grips with complete units of the Bible . . . so that it may speak as directly as possible to the more fundamental conditions and circumstances of the readers. Young children may understand few of its words, but the reality of the Biblical revelation of God may be known to them. This may be done effectively through their relationship with Christian adults who as teachers and parents recognize and experience this reality.[16]

The *Prospectus* struggles to reconcile faith and modernity. In relation to Scripture this manifests itself in attempting to reconcile a conventional view of Scripture with the contribution of the social sciences to the developmental nature of persons and with the scholarly expertise of biblical research. A recurring theme throughout is the centrality of Christ.

[T]he gospel of Jesus Christ casts a meaningful light on the canon of Scripture as a whole: God's promises to Israel, his faithfulness, the nation's breach of covenant, God's redemptive action in Christ, the New Israel and the coming of the Spirit with power, and the consummation of history in the reign of God.[17]

The Word and the Way

No new information pertaining to the nature/authority of the Bible is proffered in *The Word and the Way*. The author, Donald M. Mathers, amplifies key concepts of the *Prospectus*. Revelation, not infallibility, is the operative force in Scripture, yet not inherent revelation.

It (the Bible) is not itself revealed, it is the witness to revelation, the record of revelation, it is the testimony of the Church that God has revealed himself to his people, to the prophets, to the apostles but most of all in Jesus Christ.[18]

Scripture is not the Word of God because of any mechanical theory of infallibility, but because it is the witness to God as he has revealed himself to men.[19]

Summary statements reiterate the authority of the Bible:

[T]he Bible is the book about Jesus Christ. . . .[T]he Bible has at least the authority of an authentic record. . . . [T]he books of the Bible . . . testify and bear witness that there is a God, that he has acted in the lives of men, and that in Jesus Christ he has come in the flesh. . . . [A]s God has borne witness to himself in the past so he will bear witness to himself in the present.[20]

Junior Teacher's Guide—Year 1

The *Junior Teacher's Guide* with its focus on the Old Testament provides teachers with scholarly information under two section headings: "How the Old Testament Came to Be" and "Translation of the Bible."[21] Sandwiched between these two sections is the section "The Uniqueness of the Bible." Of immediate interest here is the location of a faith statement in the midst of biblical history. This format suggests that the uniqueness of the Bible is to be accepted as a given together with the given-ness of the oral and written tradition of the Bible.

The centrality of Christ is reiterated as the foundation of the Bible's uniqueness.

These stories are not unique in the sense that other nations do not have such tales: they are unique in the sense that they tell of Jehovah, who called Israel, to prepare for the coming of Jesus.[22]

The "covenant" theme of both testaments creates the linkage between the Old and the New, with Jesus as the one who established the new covenant. Jesus also serves as the rationale for a closed canon.

It is for this reason that the Bible is closed. Jesus has established the way of life and salvation, and we need no more for a full and satisfying life in God. Herein lies the real uniqueness of the Bible, that the old covenant finds its fulfillment in the new, and the new cannot be surpassed or rendered out of date.[23]

This statement appears contradictory to other faith statements of the *Core* curriculum pertaining to progressive revelation, that is, the "unfinished" work of the kingdom. A prime assumption of this curriculum is the possibility, indeed the reality, of God speaking to people today. There is little doubt, however, that this curriculum is a vivid illustration of the Christocentric model presented in the previous chapter.

Children's Bible Series

Joint Educational Development (JED), the umbrella organization of *Children's Bible Series,* declares the constituents for the church's educational ministry as the faith story, the faith community, and the global life-situation of people today.[24] The faith story includes the biblical story but expands to include "the witness of Christians of different racial, national and cultural traditions to what God has done within their particular histories." The biblical story is described as "the foundation of the faith story," with one of the marks of the faith community being "its recognition of the Bible as the source of its faith perspective, doctrine, and practice. . . ."[25] One of its theological and educational affirmations states as follows:

We affirm a biblical and theological rootage and style. Throughout our planning and in the educational processes and programs we may devise or advocate, we find our impetus in our faith story in the good news of God's past and continuing action in human life, mediated to us through the scriptures and uniquely in the person of Jesus of Nazareth. . . .[26]

Further reference is made to "the faith attested by the Holy Scriptures and affirmed in the confessions and life of the church, that God, incarnate in Jesus Christ and present in the Holy Spirit, wills to reconcile all persons to himself, and that God is acting in history, creating, judging, and redeeming."[27]

Within this schema the *Children's Bible Series,* as the "Knowing the Word," "Interpreting the Word," and "Living the Word," posits its purpose as "to enable persons to know the contents of the Bible and to understand their experiences and relationships in light of the biblical message."[28]

The objectives accomplished at the conclusion of this instruction (grade 6) are outlined as follows:

- Biblical skills in effectively using the Bible in individual and group study

- A discovery of the Bible speaking to issues in the lives of children
- An awareness of nine of the great biblical themes: creation; God's self-revelation; sin; judgment; redemption; people of God; providence; hope; faith-response.[29]

Specific theological affirmations are identified for "Knowing the Word" approach to Christian education:

1. Scripture is an authoritative witness for the church. The Holy Spirit inspired the authors and illumines the readers.
2. The Bible records God's revelation in Christ. It confronts persons with the promises and demands of the gospel for all of life, both personal and social.[30]

These two affirmations are most congruent with the lesson plans provided for weekly use. For example, in the *Junior Teacher's Resource Guide* "Knowing the Bible Story" (March-May 1984), the key verse to be noted in session 4 under the theme "God's Self-Revelation," is "Salvation is to be found through him alone; in all the world there is no one else whom God has given who can save us" (Acts 4:12, TEV).[31]

Again, in session 5, the key verse becomes "Believe in the Lord Jesus, and you will be saved"(Acts 16: 31, TEV).[32]

Biblical background provided in session 7 asserts that "without God's revelation in Jesus, our Creator would seem impersonal and inaccessible."[33]

The quarterly concludes with the continued sessional theme of God's self-revelation, a focus statement—"Jesus is the way to God and is the way God is known to us—and the key verse: "Jesus said . . . 'I am the way and the truth, and the life; no one comes to the Father, but by me' "(John 14:6, RSV).[34]

The authority of Scripture is illuminated in session 2 of the *Junior Teacher's Resource Guide,* (September-November 1983) "Knowing the Bible Story." Here the key verse is "All Scripture is inspired by God and is useful for teaching the truth, rebuking error, correcting faults, and giving instruction for right living" (II Timothy 3:16, TEV).[35]

A commentary follows:

The key verse expresses truth about the Scriptures. Bible inspiration is not based on its impact upon those who hear or receive it, or on those who wrote it or who transmit it, but on the fact that all Scripture is "God-breathed." These inspired Scriptures serve as an assurance for the Christian faith, and may be used as standards for teaching the truth, rebuking error, correcting faults, and restoring things to their proper place and use, and as instruction for doing what is right. . . ."[36]

This statement demonstrates a claim for inherent inspiration of Scripture and may be a discrepancy or an illumination of the above theological affirmation, that is, "the Holy Spirit inspired the authors and illumined the readers."

In summary, then, JED's approach to scriptural authority may be described as the contextual model. The "Knowing the Word" approach as illustrated through the *Children's Bible Series* is more clearly the Christocentric model edging towards ultimate authority. One critique of "Knowing the Word" identifies the context as the absent ingredient:

One weakness is a general gap between the study and the world. Few life situations are suggested at any level. The young adult resources are particularly sterile. The children's books and papers show little imagination. The absence of a bibliography gives little encouragement to adults and youth who wish to pursue a topic.[37]

Joy Curriculum

Winston Press and Harper & Row, the publishers of *Joy* curriculum, seek to provide materials attractive to many Christian denominations. An attempt is made to present the agreed upon aspects of the Christian faith "shared by all denominations, omitting doctrines, creeds, or prayers that are not shared."[38] It is not surprising, therefore, to discover the absence of a doctrinal statement pertaining to the authority of Scripture.

From a study of the overview chart and lesson plans, however, a perspective on Scripture may be inductively ascertained. For clarity purposes, statements from the overview chart have been grouped under three headings: faith claims for Scripture, statements about Jesus, and model statements.[39]

In *Joy 3* teachers' manual (for grade 3 students) further claims for Scripture are proffered:[40]

At the center of biblical faith . . . there is a sustaining trust that life bears the presence of God, that the universe is a friendly arena of trust in which God takes care of us.

[T]he Bible tells the story of God's effort to be friends with people. It contains his invitation to each of us to become his friends. It tells us about God's love for us. It tells many stories which help us understand God's love.

In the Jewish tradition, Noah's story was a foundation for understanding the ways of God.

Scripture tells us about God's care for people.

Scripture tells about the journey of people who accepted

Faith Claims for Scripture	Statements about Jesus	Model Statements
The Bible tells us how God acts in people's lives.	Jesus fulfilled many prophecies of the Hebrew scriptures, and showed that his life was part of God's plan.	Most church celebrations grew out of Bible stories about God and Jesus.
The Bible tells us that God calls us.		We base prayer on Jesus' example and other Scripture models.
The Bible records covenants between God and our faith forebears.	In Jesus as Messiah and Lord we see the full, unique revelation of God.	We include Bible verses in our prayer.
With Abraham, Moses, and Isaiah we are members of the family of God.		In the Bible and in the church we find many examples of Christian stewards.
The Bible is a source of prayer.		The Bible helps us in meditative prayer.
		We measure our decisions against values revealed in Scripture and against Jesus' command that we love one another.

change because they trusted God.
Like Abraham and Sarah, men and women in every age are called by God to risk, to change, and thus to discover a richer way of life.

[T]he events as told in Scripture contain the message that what God had done for people in the past, he continues to do for us today.

The dominant messages throughout these statements might be summarized as follows:

1. The Bible is a "faith heritage" resource; that is, it provides us with stories of our faith ancestors in the Judaeo-Christian heritage.
2. The Bible is a model or guide for Christian living.
3. The Bible is continuous revelation; for example, as God called Sarah and Abraham, God calls people today.

Throughout *Joy* the place or role of the Bible is always in the context of Piagetian child development and contemporary life experiences. The curriculum is identified as child-centered in that the focus is the child rather than content; lesson plans begin with activities or exercises related to the experience of children. The overall focus is to help children understand, primarily through experience, what it means to belong to Christian community. It is in this context and to accomplish this purpose that the Bible is used. Caution is registered in use and selection of biblical and other faith stories. In addition, tradition and current faith practices (for example, prayer and worship) are ingredients to incorporate in understanding.

We need to be careful in presenting Bible stories, explanations of doctrines, and the mysteries of faith. Young children have difficulty distinguishing reality from fantasy. They tend to focus on details and ignore the whole. They frequently associate miracles and mystery with magic. We teach the Bible to children best when we live it. . . .[41]

Joy 3 reiterates this message while acknowledging that at this stage of development, children are able "to take ownership of their scriptural heritage and adapt it for use in their own lives."[42]

In conclusion, then, the *Joy* curriculum views the Bible as "a witness to encounters between God and people, both in history and in the student's world."[43] Its foundational faith claim, expressed in lesson plans through language and experiential learning activities, is (1) our Creator loves us, gives us life, and calls us very good; (2) Jesus, God's redeeming Son, befriends us, teaches us, and calls us to become a joyful people in the power of his death and resurrection; and (3) the Spirit guides and strengthens us as we open ourselves to the prompting of God's love.

Again, we have an example of the contextual model (see illustration 4).

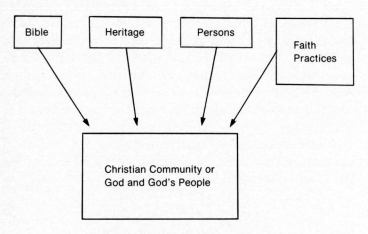

4. *Contextual Model—Joy Curriculum*

Loaves and Fishes

Loaves and Fishes is a production of the Ministry with Children Working Unit of The United Church of Canada, which developed the above theological and educational stance. Its biblical statement, therefore, is the one analysed in the theological and educational stance. An examination of one *Loaves and Fishes* resource will illustrate how this contextual model manifests itself in practice.

In the introduction, "Read Me First" contains capsuled theological and educational assumptions with one direct biblical statement:

The biblical themes reappear in our own life stories which we share with one another. These stories (the biblical and our own) connect up with a reality greater than ourselves—God.[44]

One unit of study, "A Whale of a Tale," focuses on the theme "disobedience" in response to a question asked by children: Does God still love me when I disobey? Biblical and theological background is provided for leaders with the assertion that biblical obedience and disobedience "need to be understood in the context of the covenant between God and people who believe in God—as illustrated in the . . . covenant between Yahweh and Israel," thus, equating obedience and faithfulness. The significance of the story of Jonah is viewed as "a symbol of God's persistent presence and continual challenge in our lives" and "as an illustration of the social, collective nature of sin, repentance and forgiveness."[45]

Children encounter this theme for three sessions: (1) obedience, (2) disobedience, and (3) forgiveness (Jonah and Ninevah). Each session begins with life experiences of children, followed by some aspect of the story of Jonah, and a creative expression activity to help children make connections between the biblical story and their own lives.

In another unit of study, "Blessed are the Peacemakers" becomes a response to questions of children: Will there be a third world way? If there is a nuclear war, will anyone survive? Biblical and theological background stresses the concept of "shalom" to mean "harmony, wholeness, and justice." Beginning with the first story of creation recorded in Genesis, the image becomes God's vision "of people and plants and animals living together in harmony." The writers then move to Isaiah (11:5–9), with the meaning of "shalom" being "a renewed relationship with nature;" to Micah (4:3–4) where swords are hammered into ploughs and "spears into pruning knives" and where there is time to provide food for people; to Jesus who also proclaimed shalom, calling it the "kingdom of God." The commentary concludes: "In the face of the growing threat of nuclear war, we, too, have a vision that sustains us, motivates us and helps to keep hope alive—the vision of Shalom."[46]

With this background, teachers and leaders are invited to engage with children in learning activities. Beginning with the initial goal "to get acquainted and begin to experience a sense of belonging" (through introductions and games), children then explore contemporary situations of shalom (worship prior to the learning experience highlighted the meaning of shalom— "wholeness and harmony with God and all of creation")[47] and absence of shalom through choosing appropriate pictures. In session 2, the second story of creation and the story of Noah are told to the children and dramatized by the children. Doves as symbols of shalom are made. In sessions 3 and 4, contemporary stories are told, filmstrips are shown, and information about peace organizations is shared, again, after children have the opportunity to share their personal stories about favorite TV shows and games. These contemporary learning activities are interspersed with brief stories from Scripture (for example, Isaiah and Micah). Worship both opens and closes the learning experience. At the conclusion of session 5, parents join the children for sharing and worship.

These units illustrated the working of the contextual model in practice with the interplay of children's experiences, contemporary stories, biblical and other faith stories, and worship.

To summarize, then, the four curricula presently recommended by The United Church of Canada fall within three or four models: the *Core* curriculum in the Christocentric model; *Children's Bible Series* in the Christocentric or ultimate authority model; and *Loaves and Fishes* and *Joy* in the contextual model.

While the majority of congregations use the recommended curricula, a significant minority adhere to curriculum with a fundamentalist approach to Scripture. It must also be noted that biblical theology is not the only criterion for choosing a particular curriculum. Of equal or more importance to teachers is preparation time, attractiveness of the resource, etc. The contextual model, by its very nature, demands more preparation time.

A Critical Examination

One concluding observation is that the four recommended curricula are compatible with the official historical doctrines of The United Church of Canada. Only two, however, are compatible with the theological and educational stance of the Ministry with Children Working Unit, the current agency for evaluating children's curricula. To make possible the integration of theory and practice, two options are available: (1) to revise the theological and educational stance to accommodate the three models or (2) to discontinue the recommendation of the incompatible curricula.

An exploration of the initial option elicits a further question: How reconcilable are these three models? That is, is it possible to create a doctrinal statement that validates all three models? One possibility is an "accommodation" statement. For example, formulate a statement that identifies "what is." Such a statement, however, cannot be classified as doctrinal; it is simply an analytical statement describing the practice of people. Thus, the question of reconciliation must be explored. How reconcilable, for example, are the ultimate authority and contextual model? The former elevates the Bible to unquestionable heights; the latter suggests it to be one considered resource among us. Both, as we shall observe in the following critique, demonstrate an injustice to scholarly scriptural interpretation.

A critical examination of these three identified models indicates unresolved questions pertaining to each model.

Ultimate Authority Model

In the intimate authority model, authority rests in the written word of a closed canon, claiming to contain within it inherent inspiration of God. Any challenge to biblical credibility is refuted by the invulnerable word, inspiration. Harmonization and integration of Scripture are key tasks for "the hermeneutical principle of conservative exegesis is Scriptural inerrancy, and no method or conclusion may be tolerated which would conflict with that principle."[48]

Flaws in this approach are serious:

1. Ultimate authority contradicts Christian faith that proclaims continuous revelation and, more seriously, refutes Scripture itself. That is, Scripture records encounters and confrontations of a people with God as they perceived and experienced God's ac-

tions and voice anew in ever-changing situations and epochs. Paul J. Achtemeier in *The Inspiration of Scripture* summarizes this criticism:

> If . . . the Bible is silent on the question of its own errancy, and remarkably reticent in statements about its own nature, it bears a continuing and unabating witness to the presence of God with the community of faith, shaping and guiding its life as it confronted the ever-changing situations of new historical times . . . the witness of Scripture from beginning to end points to the reality out of which Scripture grew, and within which we are to find inspiration, namely, the continuing guidance of the community of faith by God's spirit.[49]

2. The object of faith becomes the Bible, rather than God. This biblicism is a refutation of the God of the Scriptures and contradiction of the first commandment, upheld as primary by the ultimate authority school: "I am the LORD your God. . . . You shall have no other gods before me" (Exodus 20:2–3, RSV).

3. This view, for which the Bible and the Word of God are synonymous, does not recognize that sometimes for the writers of Scripture, there is no word from the Lord. For example, in I Corinthians 7:25 (RSV), the writer, credited as Paul, declares: "Now concerning the unmarried, I have no command of the Lord, but I give my opinion. . . ." Likewise, no word from the Lord is forthcoming in verse 12. Here we are confronted with "speaking personally" exhortations in an ultimate authority resource.[50]

4. In practice, those who favor the ultimate authority position are selective about what constitutes

primacy of authority. For example, the condemnation of adulterers and homosexuals as exhorted in Leviticus 20 is applauded in this view. No one would suggest, however, that physical retardation (condemned in Leviticus 21 as unholy) be included in the list of condemnations. This view possesses little or no room for contemporary insights into God's will related to these and other issues. In fact, while Scripture may be the life-giving word to many, to countless others it has been the source of oppression, as people who hold the book high often exalted racism, sexism, and other forms of oppression. Krister Stendahl comments on this critical problem of Scripture:

> How does the church live with its Bible without undesirable effects? I would guess that the last racists in this country, if ever there be an end to such, will be the ones with Bible in hand. There never has been an evil cause in the world that has not become more evident if it has been possible to argue it on biblical grounds. I think it is pretty clear that slavery in the Western world would have been overcome considerably more quickly had not slavery been part of the landscape in the Holy Book."[51]

5. With harmony and integration as presuppositions, the diversity of Scripture is abandoned. For Paul, law is bondage; for Deuteronomy, law is life abundant. Jesus is credited as saying in one situation, "Do not be angry. . . ." In another, he commits a riotous, violent act, overturning tables and substances in the Temple. James Sanders credits this diversity of Scripture to its longevity and relevance:

> Why has this Hebrew Bible lasted so long? Surely not only because there have been churches and synagogues

to pass it along, but because of its essential diversity, its own inherent refusal to absolutize any single stance as the only place where one might live under the Sovereignty of God.[52]

6. Another presupposition of this school is inerrancy. While discrepancies may be noted in translations, it is claimed that this does not mean that the original texts were in error. However, these original texts are no longer available, and what remains is a futile presupposition, uncontestable because of lack of information.

Contextual Model

The contextual model appears consistent with the development of Scripture itself. That is, scriptures were formed as people grappled with their own identity and present situations, in light of the inherited tradition—the result being new insights and theologies. For example, the concept or image of a Saviour God did not emerge from theological debate; it arose from the experience of people who understood themselves delivered or saved by God from the oppression of slavery in Egypt.

Likewise, for those favoring the contextual approach, the current experience sets the agenda and to that agenda the resources of Scripture, tradition, and the social sciences are brought. In practice, as illustrated in *Loaves and Fishes,* this means selected scriptural passages with predetermined meanings. Although attractive, this model is also found wanting.

1. The danger in decontextualizing Scripture is apparent. The prime question becomes, How does this story relate to the child (or adult)? rather than, What is its contextual meaning? Scripture does not become a corrective; rather, it is used to serve one's

own purpose. New insights that emerge from delving in depth into a Scripture passage are limited. The focus is on addressing the text, rather than being addressed by it.

2. This model demands more biblical knowledge and studies than any of its users (including the ordered ministry) possess. It suggests sufficient biblical knowledge to respond to present questions and concerns by invoking the appropriate stories/passages. This is an arduous task for the most learned among biblical students and is impractical for the format of Christian education where planning and teaching are primarily volunteer tasks.

3. It de-values a thematic understanding of Scripture and robs biblical stories of their place within a possible larger story. In this way the diversity of Scripture is upheld, but any sense of unity is minimized.

4. In this view, truth or meaning is ascertained by using a plurality of resources, including Scripture. Scripture may be a plateau higher than other resources; the suggestion, however, is the initial primacy of contemporary context consulting with Scripture. If truth is to be served, the context must live in dialogical tension with Scripture and tradition, each challenging and being challenged by the other.

Christocentric Model

Initially, the Christocentric model exhibits an uncontestable base. Christ, the foundation stone of Christianity, must be the central and prime focus of Scripture. That is, in grappling with any issue or situation, one's quest is the correct response to the imperative question, What would Jesus do/say in this situation? Jesus, the role model, becomes the determinant factor in resolving contemporary problems and solutions. Serious inadequacies are reflected, however:

1. Where Christ is the central theme in Scripture (that is, the New Testament), what is at the reader's disposal are teachings/actions ascribed to Jesus by editors and/or copiers decades after "the fact" and doctrine or theology derived from these attestations rather than "eyewitness" or biographical reports. The quest for the historical Jesus or "the historian's Jesus"[53] produced sparse material, namely, an eschatalogical worldview— "expectations that history soon would end in most dramatic ways and that the final judgment of all humankind would commence"[54]—and a sampling of parabolic sayings with open-ended meaning. While some adequate responses might be discerned with this data, it is fair to deduce that many issues and questions would remain unsolved. For the most part, in order to be decisive, we are faced with fantasizing the unknown Jesus.

2. This view renders much of Scripture as irrelevant and/or secondary. The Old Testament simply becomes background material, at its best helpful in comprehending Jesus, the Christ.

   It must also be noted that many stories and passages in the Old Testament are not related to any kind of Messiah (for example, the patriarchal and monarchy era; Psalms, Proverbs) and where they are, certainly not the kind of Messiah portrayed in Jesus, except in Isaiah 42.

3. Much of the content of the Epistles suggests that the early Christians (with only a few years of distancing from the time of Jesus) either ignored some of

Jesus' teachings or did not comprehend them. For example, Jesus, in the Gospels, is credited with recognizing and liberating women and associating with the oppressed of society; Epistle writers exhort the subservience of women in the home and church, as well as the subservience of slaves. Likewise is their interpretation of Jesus and Judaism. Stendahl amplifies:

> There was nothing un-Jewish in Jesus' critique of Judaism. It was just some good old prophetic stuff. What happened later was that his critique from within fell into alien hands and was thrown with glee by the Christians against the Jews in the Synagogue across the street. And as that critique was then combined with power—when the Christians became the more powerful and the Jews were in the minority—things went from worse to worse to worse.[55]

If such was the problem of the Early Church, how much greater is it for contemporary Christians who would know the mind and will of Christ based on historical knowledge.

The discussion of chapters 1 and 2 demonstrates that the nature and authority of the Bible as proclaimed and practiced in The United Church of Canada is exhibited through three primary models, which are traceable to its founding denominations. A critical examination of each model demonstrates its own inadequacies with each apparently incompatible with the other. That is, the ideology of the ultimate authority model is the primacy of Scripture; the Christocentric model exalts the primacy of Jesus; the contextual model exhibits the primacy of context or question.

The next task is to draw upon historical and contemporary resources in order to further enlighten understanding of biblical authority and to determine ingredients for an acceptable biblical model.

Two resources will be examined. Hans-Georg Gadamer is chosen to represent a contemporary resource for his portrayal of hermeneutical theory related to textual interpretation and historical understanding.

In the Protestant theological tradition, one scholar concerned with the reconciliation of modernity and faith was J. A. Ernesti (1707–81), a classical Lutheran theologian. A presentation and examination of his attempt to reconcile scriptural faith and modernity follows.

3. A Classical Protestant Model of Biblical Authority

The Era

Johann August Ernesti (1707–81) emerges in the milieu of the Enlightenment, a cultural environment where diverse struggles rampaged and eclectic philosophies emerged as the learned engaged in apprehending the legacies of Christianity and classical antiquity within the modern phenomenon of reason as ultimate authority. Reason challenged and, in many instances, overwhelmed traditional thought. The complexity was enhanced in that the struggle was not only between tradition and modernity but also between two facets of the ancestral heritage, that is, Christianity and classical antiquity. It was a case of adolescence struggling towards adulthood (Kant viewed the Enlightenment as "man's claim to be recognized as an adult, responsible being").[1] Authority lost its unquestionable claim, dependence upon the medieval heritage gave way to independence, and "freedom" emerged as the unifying concept.[2] History was viewed as a problematic objective reality that, subservient to reason, could be abandoned.

Pluralism abounded within the Christian church as well as in society. Deism, pietism, orthodoxy, and rationalism were major expressions of faith striving to salvage Protestant Christianity in an age of reason. With the Protestant Reformation, the Bible, as opposed to papacy and tradition, was granted unquestionable authority. Now this ultimate authority faced attack along with other accepted church doctrine. For some, such as the deists, the inspiration, revelation, and infallibility of Scripture were rejected in favor of natural religion.

The Reformation also represented a significant major shift in hermeneutics. Prior to this era, the acceptable hermeneutical system was basically the multiple-sense approach dominant since the Medieval Age, expressed through Augustine's (A.D. 354–430) theory of a fourfold sense. That is, a scriptural text has four levels of meaning: literal/historical; moral; allegorical; anagogical. The Protestant reformers reversed this position affirming that there was "one and only one" correct meaning to a text, the literal/historical meaning. Differences arose in relation to opposing interpretations. For Luther, the centrality of Scripture was Christ; thus, "where passages are unclear . . . the interpreter's task is to relate them to this Gospel." Flacius, whose *Clavius Scripturae Sacrae* (1567) marked a "landmark in the history of exegesis" as the first text on hermeneutics, deferred to *analogia fidei* (analogy of faith) as the decision-making source for discrepant passages.[3] J. A. Ernesti, in the "aftermath" of the Reformation and following the above traits, emerges as a pivotal figure for biblical hermeneutics. From the school of orthodoxy and rationalism, and in opposition to deism and pietism, he willingly placed Scripture under the principles for all interpretation but within the faith claims of Lutheran orthodoxy. Ernesti confronted Scripture with the intention of creating intelligibility and credibility for a learned people of reason.

The purpose of this chapter is to examine Ernesti's biblical hermeneutic and basis for scriptural authority as contained in *Principles of Interpretation* (a translation of *Institutio Interpretis Novi Testamenti*), criticize his findings, and suggest further directions in the search for scriptural authority and a biblical hermeneutic.

The Person

Because Ernesti is largely unknown to the North American audience, brief biographical data will introduce him to the reader. Born in Thuringa, Germany, he was educated at Schulpforta, Wittenberg, and Leipzig where he lived for fifty years. Besides being a German Lutheran theologian, he was a classical scholar with an exceptional command of the Greek language. A human interest incident recorded in *A History of Classical Scholarship* relates that "he was already reading to himself in class the last book of Herodian, while the master was slowly expounding the first."[4] By the age of thirty-two he had completed six volumes of Cicero. For twenty-two of his fifty years at Leipzig he was professor of theology; he also held the positions of principal and professor of eloquence.[5]

Strongly influenced by the development of rationalism and classical philology, J. A. Ernesti, then, was an ecclesiastic, scholar, and writer. (Actually, *A History of Classical Scholarship* describes him as "superficial as a writer, but intelligent as an expositor.")[6] *Institutio Interpretis Novi Testamenti* is cited as his most important work[7] and a "landmark in the history of hermeneutics."[8] One reason for these claims is that Friedrich Ast (1778–1841) and Friedrich August Wolf (1759–1824), two forerunners of Friedrich Schleiermacher, use Ernesti's elements for grammatical interpretation as their foundation.[9] Another, as we will observe later, is that conservative Christianity found a strong ally in Ernesti's attempt to reconcile orthodoxy and rationalism.

Various works contain snippets of information about

Ernesti, creating curiosity in an inquisitive mind. R. E. Palmer in *Hermeneutics* quotes Ernesti's revolutionary statement: "The verbal sense of Scripture must be determined in the same way in which we ascertain that of other books."[10] (Actually, similar statements were made by the controversial deists, for example, Anthony Collins).[11] Conservative Milton Terry in *Biblical Hermeneutics* describes him as "probably the most distinguished name in the history of exegesis in the eighteenth century."[12] Edgar Krentz in *The Historical-Critical Method,* borrowing a phrase from Franz Lau, describes him as the "father of the profane scientific interpretation of the Bible."[13] (*The Eclipse of Biblical Narrative* attributes the phrase as that of Emmanuel Hirsh in relation to Ernesti.)[14]

A direct examination of Ernesti's own work will amplify some of the above statements and ascertain the extent of his success in reconciling tradition and rationalism.

Ernesti's Biblical Hermeneutic

For the purpose of clarity, Ernesti's biblical hermeneutic is described under various headings. For this chapter's purpose, Ernesti's most crucial and controversial presupposition is section 31 of his work:

The principles of interpretation are common to sacred and profane writings. Of course, the Scriptures are to be investigated by the same rules as other books.[15]

Theme

The central concern of this hermeneutic is to maintain the integrity of and reconcile orthodoxy and rationalism.

Definitions

Diverging from the multiple-sense approach to Scripture (that is, a passage that may have more than one meaning) of the Roman church, Ernesti, in faithful Reformation style, argues for a single-sense approach;[16] that is, a passage must have one correct meaning. This single-sense approach manifests itself in the definition of hermeneutics and the art of interpretation:

Hermeneutics is the science which teaches to find, in an accurate and judicious manner, the meaning of an author, and appropriately to explain it to others.[17]

The art of interpretation is the art of teaching what is the meaning of another's language; or that skill, which enables us to attach to another's language the same meaning that the author himself attached to it.[18]

If two passages contradict each other, the text of one must be faulty.[19]

Elements of Interpretation

To identify the scholarly requirements for correct interpretation, Ernesti uses the phrase *subtilitas intelligendi et explicandi* (skill in understanding and skill in explanation). Here skill is synonymous with accuracy.[20] These technical skills are obtained through the mastery of languages, philology, theology, and philosophy.

Evidence of "subtilitas intelligendi et explicandi"

Several questions are posed to determine skill in interpretation.

- Does the interpreter understand the passage?
- If not, does the interpreter understand the barriers that prevent understanding?
- Does the interpreter have a "proper method of investigating the sense of those passages which are difficult?"[21]
- Can the interpreter express in the author's original language or another language using sound argument

and illustration, the author's intended meaning?
- Does the interpreter have purity of diction while maintaining the original features ascertained through the text?[22]

Principles of Interpretation

These principles can be summarized by identifying two major avenues or claims in ascertaining the correct meaning of Scripture.

The "usus loquendi": By this phrase Ernesti means "the sense which usage (of words) attaches to the words of any language."[23] Basic to this technique is the claim that "every word must have some meaning."[24] Indeed, Ernesti agrees that a word may have different meanings but the correct meaning in relation to a particular text is derived from the *usus loquendi.*[25] Scrupulous attention and research into all influences on the language of the author is necessitated by this phrase, for example, culture, history, religion, education, origin of word, text, etc.[26] For scriptural interpretation, knowledge of Hebrew and Greek is an essential prerequisite as is, in the New Testament, knowledge of the dialect of the writer.[27] This enterprise results in ascertaining the literal (verbal), grammatical, historical, and linguistic sense of words, which, to Ernesti, are one and the same. He explains:

The observance of all these matters belongs in a special manner to grammarians, whose business it is to investigate the sense of words. Hence the literal sense is also called the grammatical; literalis and grammaticus having the same meaning. It is also called the historic sense; because, like other matters of fact, it is supported by historic testimony.[28]

In emphasizing the priority of this principle, Ernesti reiterates Melanchthon: "The Scripture cannot be understood theologically until it is understood grammatically."[29]

Analogy of Faith:

Ernesti's claim, in this regard, is that the doctrine of the church has been derived from Scripture and should, therefore, guide interpretation of it.[30] This provides for accurate interpretation and preservation of the faith.

Grammatical analogy is the rule of speaking, or form of speech, constituted by the laws of language. . . . In like manner, the analogy of sacred doctrine or faith consists in the summary of religion, and the rules plainly taught in the Scriptures; whence the Latin church called it "regula fidei." To this analogy all things are to be referred, so that nothing may be discordant with it. And when this is done, the analogy of faith is said to be preserved.[31]

This theory of Ernesti's finds support with Flacius and Augustine as outlined in the introductory paragraphs.

Schema

To understand the author's intended meaning and, thus, the meaning of a text, a reconstruction of the original text is required. This occurs through various steps:

- Through direct and indirect testimony (where the original language is now "dead," direct testimony comes from those who had firsthand experience with the language when it was a "living" one or from those who have mastered the written language during the language's era. Indirect testimony is derived from examining the larger design or context of the passage)[32]
- By comparison of words and grammatical usage[33]
- By grammatical analogy with the same and kindred languages[34]
- By appeal to the "nature of things"—innate conceptions, common sense, and the plain elements of knowledge[35]

- By comparison of derived results with accepted church doctrine[36]

Rationale

Divine inspiration is the basic claim of Ernesti's argument for a single-sense hermeneutic, that of the author's intended meaning. Here, too, lies the authority of Scripture.

As the books of Scriptures were written by men divinely inspired, it is evident there can be no real contradiction in them. God is not incapable of seeing what is consistent, and what is contradictory; nor can he forget, when he speaks, what was said on former occasions. . . . For the very reason that these books are inspired, every interpretation ought to agree with the design of the writer, or harmonize with the context. . . . We admit this principle in the interpretation of profane writers; much more ought we to admit it in respect to the Scriptures. Mere men, through negligence or want of knowledge, may insert some things that disagree with their principal design; but not so the Holy Spirit.[37]

The "divine inspiration" argument is also his rationale for new words in the New Testament.

These words, by the way, were not invented by the apostles, and could not have been; for such invention is a thing that belongs to minds trained up by literary discipline, and not to unlettered men. We may conclude, therefore, that terms of such a kind were suggested by the Holy Spirit; which is an argument in favor of the divine inspiration of the Scriptures.[38]

Ernesti's argument may be outlined as follows: God, who inspired the writers of Scripture, is the author of Scripture. God does not contradict himself; therefore, there is one intended meaning to passages of Scripture, that of the author, inspired by God.

This argument, in addition to opposing traditional Roman church interpretation, was intended to combat contemporary mysticism and pietism or "uncritical rationalism."[39]

Ernesti himself notes the

Error of those who affirm that the words of Scripture mean all that they possible can mean. This sprung from the Rabbinical schools, and passed from them, in early times, to Christians. The transition is very easy from this error to every kind of license in the introduction of allegory, prophecy, and mystery, into every part of the Bible. . . .[40]

A Critical Examination

Ernesti's principles and elements of hermeneutics, with their strong emphasis on mastery of languages and scholarly knowledge of biblical literature, theology, and philosophy as prerequisites for acquiring the art of interpretation, are technical, intentional, and sound. They take seriously the depth and scope of the hermeneutical enterprise and demonstrate that criticism is a corrective to a laissez-faire approach to interpretation and safeguard to nonabusiveness in interpretation. It is in the area of biblical hermeneutics that inadequacies are identified. Ernesti's presupposition that rationalism and faith (or orthodoxy and reason) could be reconciled was, it appears, a barrier to objective interpretation and correct meaning. The following paragraphs demonstrate how this conviction produces problematic results.

Ernesti's rationale for a single-sense hermeneutic of the "author's intended meaning" is grounded in the authority of Scripture, as outlined in the above argument. This authority rests in the uncontradictory nature of God as the source of inspiration, as stated in premise 2. The inadequacy of this argument is multidimensional. In relation to the argument, God as author of Scripture is neither defendable nor debatable. The premise is refutable from a scientific examination. Those who uphold the conviction, however, claim that where conflict between science and Scripture authentically occurs, science, not Scripture, is in error. What is more problematic is the second premise of God's uncontradictory nature and, thus, one intended meaning. To hold these claims results in the impossibility of ascertaining the author's intended meaning. There are many discrepant passages in Scripture; these discrepancies are frequently highlighted, rather than diminished, by a critical approach. One passage may be faulty, but which one? Pushing that query to exhaustion, the conclusion becomes, "God only knows!" Ernesti neglects the human processes through which revelation filters: from the minds of the original recipients, to the original writers or collators, to the editors, to the translators, to the interpreters. To quote Ernesti, God may not forget "when he speaks, what was said on former occasions,"[41] but humanity, the vehicle through which inspiration is channeled, does.

Ernesti's argument is also problematic in relation to other claims:

1. His visionary assertion that the Bible must be treated as any other book does not manifest itself in practice. Claiming God as supreme author automatically places the Bible on a different plateau from other texts.
2. In an attempt to reconcile criticism and tradition, Ernesti recommends the "principle of confirmation." That is, is the derived meaning congruent with Church doctrine? If not, it appears that the meaning is the correct one.

A paradox is, thus, created. On the one hand, Ernesti promotes a *tabula rasa* in approaching a text in order to understand it linguistically. On the other hand, he advocates church doctrine, which was derived from Scripture, as the guide to interpretation, and, in turn, the results obtained from interpretation must be compatible with this doctrine. In addition to ambiguity, this approach entangles the interpreter in a hermeneutical circle; the interpreter ends where she or he began! Further problematical questions in this area are, How is faith challenged? How is faith embraced as one's own without critique? How do new insights emerge if the purpose of the enterprise is to support the previously held faith stance?

Ernesti's legacy and usefulness as a resource in hermeneutics for this discussion was his insistence on the grammatical/historical element in interpretation, a task requiring meticulous scholarly attention by the interpreter, whose task is to become the transparent activator of the texts' meaning while speaking out of a tradition and community (analogy of faith). He demonstrates, through his elements and principles of interpretation, the seriousness of the hermeneutical endeavour in interpreting Scripture. His usefulness is also demonstrated in historical demarcation. That is, Ernesti marks the possible ending of the Reformation process in relation to the historical-critical method, for, following Ernesti, Schleiermacher (1768– 1834) heralds a new shift in the hermeneutical endeavour, with emphasis on *Geisteswissenschaften* (knowledge of the spirit), the *Geist* (spirit) of humankind, and the emphasis on the author, rather than text. The process of interpretation becomes a communion between interpreter and author.

Eighteenth-century orthodoxy and rationalism intertwined in that orthodoxy adopted the rationalistic approach while rationalism attempted to preserve orthodoxy.[42]

Ernesti's hermeneutic illuminated in *Principles of Interpretation* illustrates how aptly he is a product of and contributor to this theological/scientific milieu. The presupposition was that a critical approach would substantiate the authority of Scripture, and orthodox rationalists, like Ernesti, determined to prove the validity and accuracy of this premise.[43] It was his scientific elaboration of scriptural interpretation, common to all texts, that earned him the title of "father of the profane scientific interpretation of the Bible.[44] Edgar Krentz differentiates this title from that of "father of historical-critical theology" (accredited to Johan Salomo Semler, 1725–91) because of Ernesti's scriptural sense, that is, the inerrancy of inspired Scripture.[45] Conservative Christianity found a strong ally in this attempt of Ernesti to reconcile orthodoxy and rationalism.

This chapter demonstrates, however, that to be faithful to text and credible to rational humanity, the authority of Scripture demands different criteria than that of verbal inspiration and inerrancy. As biblical fallibility was deemed an inadequate argument for abandoning Christian faith and authority of Scripture, so biblical infallibility is inadequate proof for upholding it.

Questions still linger: How does one reconcile Scripture and the scientific enterprise? By what criteria does one uphold the authority of Scripture?

Advances in historical, literary, canonical, and textual criticism since the days of Ernesti are beneficial aids in this enterprise. The rise of liberal theology in the nineteenth century resulted in greater historical research. In biblical hermeneutics, distinctions were made between the "Jesus of history" and the "Christ of faith." The quest for the historical Jesus in the late nineteenth and early twentieth centuries became a major concern. Albert Schweitzer's *Von Reimarus Zu Wrede* (translated as *The Quest of the Historical Jesus*) published in 1906 is representative of this research.[46]

One further major development is the recognition of subjectivity in the scientific endeavor. That is, Ernesti imaged a text as an object, with an unbiased interpreter approaching the text objectively to ascertain the correct meaning. Recent positions, represented by Hans-Georg Gadamer, recognize the subjectivity of both text and interpreter and encourage a dialogical relationship between both. The interpreter addresses the text and the text addresses the interpreter. Through this ongoing hermeneutical dialogue, meanings of the text are ascertained, necessitating a multiple-sense approach. It is on Gadamer's work that we now focus attention.

4. A Textual Model of Biblical Authority

Socrates: Unless either philosophers begin to rule as kings in the cities or those who are now called kings and bosses start doing philosophy genuinely and adequately, until there is a conjunction of these two things—philosophy and political power—while the motley crew of those who at present pursue one or the other separately is compulsorily excluded, until then there will be no end to troubles for our states, my dear Glaucon, nor, I think, for the human race either . . . .

Glaucon: Whom do you mean then by the true philosophers?

Socrates: Those who love to contemplate the spectacle of truth.[1]

Hans-Georg Gadamer, in true philosophical tradition, contemplates and proffers an effective-historical, dialectic interpretative method, a persuasive refutation of the hermeneutical scientific methodology of the Enlightenment and, thus, of Ernesti.

The Argument

In the "one and many" debate of textual interpretation, Gadamer argues for multiplicity of meaning:

There cannot . . . be any one interpretation that is correct "in itself," precisely because every interpretation is concerned with the text itself. . . . Every interpretation has to adapt itself to the hermeneutical situation to which it belongs.[2]

In view of the finite nature of our historical existence there is something absurd about the whole ideal of a uniquely correct interpretation.[3]

Elaborating further Gadamer points to derived textual meaning as the result of one's questions, prejudices, and interests.[4] These concerns differ from age to age.[5]

Tracing and critiquing problems posited by hermeneutics through the philosophical thought of Schleiermacher, Dilthey, Husserl, and Heidegger, Gadamer develops a new hermeneutic, based on a phenomenological approach to "understanding" and a supportive argument to demonstrate "that understanding is never subjective behavior toward a given "object," but towards its effective-history—the history of its influence; in other words, understanding belongs to the being of that which is understood. . . ."[6] "Effective-historical consciousness," thus, becomes a powerful worldview concept in his thesis, claiming that "the element of effective-history is operative in all understanding of tradition."[7]

The substance of Gadamer's hermeneutic is outlined as follows.

Theme

Gadamer's theme is a human historical sciences (*Geisteswissenschaften*) hermeneutic based on an understanding of humanity and a linguistic worldview.

Primary Questions

The primary questions of Gadamer's hermeneutic include

- What is understanding?
- How is understanding possible?
- What are the conditions in which understanding takes place?

Claims

The claims of Gadamer's hermeneutic include the following.

Humanity is finite. Based on this premise, the logical conclusion is the impossibility of totality of meaning, the givenness of prejudice, and the "absurdity" of "one correct interpretation."[8]

Existence is historical. Here the meaning of history is perceived, not as objective events of the past, but rather as that which we presently live within. Humanity both produces history and is produced by it.[9] Acceptance of this worldview results in a negation of texts as objective entities of the past, separated by temporal distance from the interpreter. With both text and interpreter living within history, application becomes integral to interpretation "for the text is part of the whole of tradition in which the age takes an objective interest and in which it seeks to understand itself."[10]

The world is linguistic in nature. Supporting Wilhelm von Humboldt's primary contribution to the hermeneutical field, namely, that a view of language is a view of the world,[11] Gadamer clarifies:

Language is not just one of man's possessions in the world, but on it depends the fact that man has a world at all . . . this world is linguistic in nature. . . . Not only is the world "world" only insofar as it comes into language, but language, too, has its real being only in the fact that the world is represented within it.[12]

This philosophical insight serves to differentiate between the animal and human world. Insofar as "communication . . . is a living process in which a community of life is lived out" humans and animals possess a commonality, the differing quality being that in the communicative language of humans, "world is disclosed."[13]

To provide further credence for his hermeneutic, Gadamer illustrates with the image of the mastery of another language; that is, "you understand a language by living in it."[14] In this accomplishment, however, two factors are noted:

1. Awareness of another worldview results from the usage of language through conversation or literary study rather than from the technical learning of a language.
2. In the development of another worldview, one forgets neither one's language nor worldview.[15] This linguistic worldview concept, thus, recognizes language as the "universal medium in which understanding itself is realised."[16]

These philosophical claims provide the pivotal foundation for further argument to challenge the scientific methodology of the Enlightenment as inappropriate for a hermeneutic of the human sciences.

Theory

Constituents in the hermeneutical enterprise as tendered by Gadamer are the *text* and the *interpreter,* both living within the historical traditions, both in the dialectic of producing and being produced by history. The hermeneutical task is to ascertain, through the continuous process of question and response, the meaning of the text.

In support of this hermeneutic and in criticism of a scientific methodology, six primary concerns are addressed: prejudice, temporal distance, tradition, concept of questions, application, and language.

Prejudice

Drawing upon a prior, positive definition of "prejudice," (namely, "a judgment that is given before all the elements that determine a situation have been finally examined[17]") before the Enlightenment ascribed to it negativity of meaning, Gadamer recognizes "prejudice" as the starting point in the hermeneutical task. The initial queries posited to a text are prejudicial questions; these questions partially determine the textual meaning. But, argues Gadamer, "a person trying to understand a text is prepared for it to tell him something . . . The important thing is to be aware of one's own bias, so that the text may present itself in all its newness and thus be able to assert its own truth against one's own foremeanings."[18] The Enlightenment's fallacy was the universal removal of all prejudice, an impossible task because of humanity's finite historical nature, and, thus, a prejudice in itself.[19] A more authentic approach is to distinguish between legitimate and illegitimate prejudices. This, however, cannot be accomplished in advance by an objective methodology—it is accomplished in the process of understanding.

The prejudices and fore-meanings in the mind of the interpreter are not at his free disposal. He is not able to separate in advance the productive prejudices that hinder understanding and lead to misunderstandings. This separation . . . must take place in the understanding itself, and hence hermeneutics must ask how it happens. But this means it must place in the foreground what has remained entirely peripheral in previous hermeneutics: temporal distance and its significance for understanding.[20]

Addressing the prejudicial concern brings to the foreground another debated issue in hermeneutics, that of temporal distance.

Temporal Distance

Time, often viewed in the hermeneutical task as a barrier, is highlighted "as a positive and productive possibility of

understanding."[21] Time is the ingredient in the hermeneutical endeavour that enables one to distinguish between true and false prejudices[22] and, thus, to ascertain
the true meaning of a text, recognizing that true meaning
is "an infinite process."[23]

Tradition

In the Enlightenment, reason was the only acceptable authority. In its critique of such claim, Romanticism de-
fended tradition as undebatable authority, recognizing
that "that which has been sanctioned by tradition and
custom has an authority that is nameless, and our finite
historical being is marked by the fact that always the authority of what has been transmitted—and not only what
is clearly grounded—has power over our attitudes and
behaviour."[24] While supporting this contribution of Romanticism, Gadamer's critique is of both the Enlightenment and Romanticism. Not all acquiescence to authority
is synonymous to "blind obedience," he asserts. Instead,
in relation to persons the essence of authority constitutes
recognition and knowledge—"knowledge, namely, that
the other is superior to oneself in judgment and insight
and that for this reason his judgment takes precedence,
that is, it has priority over one's own."[25] The correlation
of authority, thus, is knowledge rather than obedience.[26]
On the other hand, tradition is not sacrosanct. "Even the
most genuine and solid tradition . . . needs to be affirmed, embraced, cultivated . . . preservation is as much
a freely-chosen action as revolution and renewal."[27] Recognizing also tradition as living ("we stand always within
tradition"),[28] the process of understanding must acknowledge reciprocity of relationship where tradition
both addresses and is addressed by the interpreter. "Understanding is not to be thought of so much as an action
of one's subjectivity, but the placing of oneself within a

process of tradition, in which past and present are constantly fused."[29]

The Concept of Question

The paramount significance of "question" finds its foundation in the Socratic view of knowledge. "I do not think that I know what I do not know."[30] Knowledge, then, begins with recognition of one's ignorance and a desire to know. Ignorance is alleviated and knowledge is developed through the art of questioning, a dialectical process in that response to questioning evokes further questioning. Gadamer describes this as "the openness of the question."[31] Lest one deem this as a simplistic or chaotic process, Gadamer, again evoking the Socratic dialogues, identifies the difficulty in asking "true" questions. "It is more difficult to ask questions than to answer them."[32] Here "horizon" becomes a key concept in criteria—horizon meaning "the range of vision that includes everything that can be seen from a particular vantage point."[33] Openness in question is not equated with limitlessness; the boundaries are the "horizon" of the question. No fixed criteria determine appropriate "horizon," but obvious examples are cited as incompatible with openness. These are (a) the pedagogical question where the expected answer is previously determined; (b) the rhetorical question where there is no expected response; (c) the distorted question where the response is impossible; and (d) the "false" question based on false presuppositions and pretense to openness.[34]

A text is a response to question. Texts, thus, pose questions to the interpreter, reversing the question and answer process.[35]

The voice that speaks to us from the past—be it text, work, trace—itself poses a question and places our meaning in openness. In order to answer this question, we, of whom the question is asked, must ourselves begin to ask questions. We must attempt to reconstruct the question to which the transmitted text is the answer.[36]

This reciprocal, dialectic relationship between text and interpreter continues until "fusion of the horizons" occurs; that is, "we regain the concepts of a historical past in such a way that they also include our comprehension of them."[37]

The superiority of question in the hermeneutical process reemphasizes the argument against scientific methodology for a human sciences hermeneutic. Gadamer summarizes:

The priority that the question holds in knowledge shows in the most basic way the limitedness of the idea of method for knowledge from which our argument as a whole has proceeded. There is no such thing as a method of learning to ask questions, of learning to see what needs to be questioned. . . . All questioning and desire to know presuppose a knowledge that one does not know; so much so, indeed, that it is a particular lack of knowledge that leads to a particular question.

Plato, unforgettably, shows wherein the difficulty lies in the way of knowing what we do not know. It is the power of opinion against which it is so hard to obtain an admission of ignorance. It is opinion that suppresses questions.[38]

Application

Traditionally, hermeneutics was comprised of three distinct elements: understanding; interpretation; and application. Application in this sense meant its meaning for a particular situation or people after universal or original meaning of the text was derived. Theological and legal hermeneutics were dependent upon application in this manner.

Gadamer argues for all three comprising "one unified process."[39] Application now becomes integral to the hermeneutical act of understanding, for understanding consists of the interpreter within his or her tradition engaging a text in its tradition. Thus, distinction between universal and particular meaning is diffused, for both are enmeshed, and the actual meaning of the text includes both.[40]

Language

Gadamer's linguistic worldview leads naturally to a linguistic hermeneutical process— language being the universal medium through which understanding occurs.[41] As one inherits a new linguistic world through learning another language, so one, in interpretation, seeks to apprehend the linguistic world of the text. This framework of reference enables Gadamer to speak of "the work of hermeneutics as a conversation with the text . . . thus, that which is handed down in literary form is brought back out of the alienation in which it finds itself and into the living presence of conversation, whose fundamental procedure is always question and answer."[42] Gadamer also refers to "making the text speak"[43] and understanding as "an encounter with something that asserts itself as truth"[44]—expressions that further support a world and, thus, a hermeneutic grounded in language. Gadamer's analogy for textual understanding is that of two people in conversation, a characteristic of which is openness to the other where one "gets inside the other to such an extent that he understands not a particular individual, but what he says."[45] Gadamer acknowledges, however, a breakdown in this analogy: "Texts are 'permanently fixed expressions of life' which have to be understood, and that means that one partner in the hermeneutical conversation, the text, is expressed only through the other partner, the interpreter."[46] The purpose, however, is similar, namely, in conversation, to understand what a person says; in text, to understand the meaning of the text.

Summary

Gadamer's developed theory of understanding resulting from the above deliberations is as follows. History, tradition, and language are not separate entities belonging to our past that can be objectively analysed. They are part of our "being," "functioning simultaneously in three modes of temporality: past, present, and future."[47] We understand from within history, from our particular time and place.

Implications for Biblical Understanding

A serious consideration of Gadamer's hermeneutic for biblical understanding necessitates adequate support for the following:

- The primacy of the "encounter" motif within Scripture
- Acknowledging a prejudicial approach to Scripture; being open to the "horizon" of question.
- An integrative historical view; that is, past, present and future interwoven

The Primacy of the "Encounter" Motif within Scripture

"Encounter between God and the people of God" is an uncontested umbrella theme of Scripture. Some would argue that these encounters are historical fact, while others vouch for their legendary, mythic, and/or poetic nature, and diverse interpretations result from these conflicting approaches. Accordingly, diversity abounds concerning the authority or mandate of these encounters for contemporary people of faith, with some vouching for direct application and others valuing the approach of the humanities; that is, these encounters broaden and enrich modernity's horizons of the human story. The "encounter" motif, with its multiplicity of context and motivation, however, is upheld.

Recurring vignettes throughout Scripture are those of discerning divine will through struggling, wrestling, soul searching, questioning, and/or debate. According to the Yahwistic tradition ("J") "Jacob" is renamed "Israel" (meaning "one who strives or contends with God") as a result of a strenuous but victorious wrestle with God (Genesis 32:22–29). In the same tradition, Sarah's response to hearing the Word announce the imminent birth of a son in her and Abraham's old age is laughter, followed by denial of laughter and recurring laughter when the birth occurred. "God has given me cause to laugh; all those who hear of it will laugh with me" (Genesis 21:6, JB).

Similarly, other major biblical heroes actively encounter the Divine in order to apprehend the Word. The fallacy of the adage "the patience of Job" is apparent as one confronts in the Book of Job forty-one chapters of questioning, denial, and argument with God and friends who claim infallible knowledge of God as Job seeks explanation and interpretation of his never-ending woes. Towards the end of the encounter Job hears the Word: "Brace yourself like a fighter, now it is my turn to ask questions and yours to inform me" (Job 40:7, JB). Job appears as a challenge to the contemporary and traditional theology of the time that disaster is a direct result of sin. If that is so, what about the suffering of the innocent, queries Job.

The dilemma of "Israel in exile" in 587 B.C. surrounding Yahweh's word(s) for foreign situations is captured in the poignant words of Psalm 137:

Beside the streams of Babylon
we sat and wept
at the memory of Zion,
leaving our harps
hanging on poplars . . .
How could we sing
one of Yahweh's hymns
in a pagan country?

(Psalm 137:1–2, 4, JB)

For hitherto (for example, during the monarchy) Yahweh could only be worshipped in Israel as Yahweh's sovereignty did not extend beyond these boundaries. Thus, we have a report of Naaman the Syrian attempting to rectify the situation by moving earth from Israel to Rimmon (II Kings 5:17, 18).

Likewise for Jesus in the garden of Gethsemane there is no clear insight or direction from the tradition for the next steps on his journey. Phrases used to describe this dilemma of "no word from the Word" are "a sudden fear came over him, and great distress" (Mark 14:34, JB) and "his sweat fell to the ground like great drops of blood" (Luke 22:44, JB).

New stories and new understanding of stories from the heritage developed as biblical people encountered the Divine through immense struggle to determine appropriate and faithful response for new questions on untrodden paths.

Some of these pivotal questions, situations and solutions are as follows:

Question	Situation	Solution
How do we preserve our identity as followers of Yahweh and survive in an agricultural setting?	Conquest of Canaan (ca. 1220 B.C.E.) moving from being a nomadic people to a settled people	"Yahweh alone" theology. Hitherto other gods were viewed as rivals ("You shall have no other gods before me." Exodus 20:3) Now Yahweh is One, transcendent, unique.
How do we sing the Lord's song in a strange land? How shall we live? What now is our identity?	Destruction of the Temple and Babylonian Exile 587 B.C.E.	Israel-in exile, namely, the priestly editors, reviewed their tradition (known as the P tradition) in light of this crisis and molded and shaped the Yahwistic(J), Elohistic(E), Deuteronomical(D) and Priestly(P) traditions into the heritage of Judaism.
How can we survive in the midst of Hellenistic invasions, Temple raids, banning of our laws and observances?	Persecution of Antiochus Epiphanes IV, Edict of 167 B.C.E.	Apocalyptic literature. Yahweh's rule will be manifested over all the earth and the covenant will be fulfilled.

continues on page 74

Question	Situation	Solution
How do we live without the visible symbol of Yahweh's presence and acceptance in our midst?	Destruction of the Temple, A.D. 70.	Apocalyptists—Wait Essenes—isolated community life Christians—Jesus becomes chief priest; Church replaces Temple. Pharisees— one acts in daily life "as if" one were a temple priest. The whole of life (people, land, community) becomes holy.
How does a Gentile, not born of Jewish flesh, become true Israel?	Spread of Christianity from Jewish to Gentile soil	Some aspects of Law not binding for Gentile Christians.

Prejudicial Approach to Scriptures

In using "prejudice" as an appropriate approach to Scripture, I am employing it in the positive sense posited by Gadamer, as perspective, frame of reference, or under-lying assumptions. The undeniable prejudicial approach to Scripture is evident throughout its pages. Some biblical authors/editors state explicitly in writing:

"The time has come . . . and the Kingdom of God is close at hand. Repent and believe the Good News."

(Mark, 1:15, JB)

(For most New Testament scholars this passage summa-rizes the primary message of Jesus.)

These are recorded so that you may believe that Jesus is the Christ, the Son of God.

(John 20:31, JB)

This news is about the Son of God who, according to the human nature he took, was a descendent of David: it is about Jesus Christ our Lord who . . . was proclaimed Son of God in all his power through his resurrection from the dead.

(Romans 1:3–4, JB)

In other books prejudice is inherent in the message:

Yahweh said to Abram, ". . . I will make you a great nation; I will bless you and make your name so famous that it will be used as a blessing."

(Genesis 12:1–2, JB)

"My father was a wandering Armaean. He went down into Egypt to find refuge there, few in numbers; but there he became a nation, great, mighty and strong. The Egyptians illtreated us, they gave us no peace and inflicted harsh slavery on us. But we called on Yahweh the God of our fathers. Yahweh heard our voices and saw our misery, our toil and our oppression; and Yahweh brought us out of Egypt with mighty hand and outstretched arm, with great terror, and with signs and wonders. He brought us here and gave us this land, a land where milk and honey flow.

(Deuteronomy 26:5–9, JB)

This is the revelation given by God to Jesus Christ so that he could tell his servants about the things which are now to take place very soon; he sent his angel to make it known to his servant John, and John had written down everything he saw and swears it is the word of God guaranteed by Jesus Christ.

(Revelation 1:1– 2, JB)

These prejudices or pre-understandings contained in Scripture are essential aids in framing parameters or "horizon" of appropriate questioning for exacting the meaning of the text. Two pivotal questions in relation to the Old and New Testament respectively are, What did it mean to be "Israel" in the various traditions (J,E,D,P)? and, What did it mean to be "Christian" in the biblical era? Subsequent questions naturally follow:

- How did they view themselves?
- How did they view others (other sects, the normative religion, outsiders)?
- What were the questions and situations that formulated their views about God, world, humanity, purpose in life, etc.?
- How did others respond?
- Were the solutions offered adequate for people in general?
- How influential were they?
- What do we know about the Jesus of history?
- What do we know about the Christ of faith?

A probing exploration of these questions moves the interpreter to further questioning related to history, institutions, languages, culture, and literature of the era. It is in this spiral of question and answer, answer and question—that is, "addressing and being addressed by the text"–that meaning occurs. Likewise, identifying the prejudice of the text focuses questions that are beyond the "horizon" and, thus, unacceptable. For example, the philosophical question of the reality of God is incongruent with Scripture for the reality of the Divine is one of Scripture's major presuppositions. In a similar way, approaching the nativity stories of Jesus for a scientific analysis of immaculate conception is beyond the horizon of the text. Appropriate questioning might include the query, Why did the authors/editors determine that "Jesus" required a "virgin" birth? Likewise, proof texting to support a contemporary issue is outside the "horizon," for proof texting removes text from context.

Canon

A canon begins to take shape first and foremost because a question of identity or authority has arisen and a canon begins to become unchangeable or invariable somewhat later, after the question of identity has for the most part been settled.[48]

The relevance of the Hebrew scriptures to the above quote has already been observed. Another catastrophic event, the second destruction of the Temple in A.D. 70, hastened and finalized the Hebrew canon. At Yavneh, ca. A.D. 90, the gathering place of the Pharisees and other Jewish groups after A.D. 70, Jewish leaders revised, selected, and determined from a myriad of writings those to be valued as authoritative for communities of faith. This "valuing" process underscores the prejudicial factor in canonization. All sacral literature was not included, the criterion apparently being those writings assessed or experienced as life giving in the midst of death blows or those writings most conducive to preserving and reestablishing identity in the midst of identity threats. The prominence of historical/contextual selection is highlighted in this understanding of canon as well as the rationale for canonical authority. Torah replaced Temple as the central symbol of faith.

Similar claims are made for canonization of the New Testament. The archeological treasures discovered near Nag 'Hammadi in 1945 produced "some fifty-two texts from the early centuries of the Christian era--including a collection of early Christian gospels, previously unknown. Besides the Gospel of Thomas and the Gospel of Philip, the find included the Gospel of Truth and the Gospel to the Egyptians. . . . Another group of texts consists of writings attributed to Jesus' followers, such as the secret book of James, the Apocalypse of Paul, the letter of Peter to Philip, and the Apocalypse of Peter."[49]

No definitive dates are cited for the closure of New Testament canon. Robert W. Funk in *Parables and Presence* refers to the mid-fourth century A.D as the date that canon signified the Old and New Testaments, noting that the "Council of Laodicea in Phrygia (about 360), Canon 59 speaks of both uncanonical and the canonical books of the old and new covenants" and that around "350 C.E. Athanasius spoke of the Shepherd of Hermas as uncanonical."[50] Paul J. Achtemeier in *The Inspiration of Scripture* cites the Synods of Hippo (A.D. 393) and Carthage (A.D. 397) as dates for canonization. The Syrian church, however, did not accept this canon. For the Protestant church, the canon of Scripture was formalized during the Reformation.[51]

It is known, however, that several pivotal events compelled canonical activity: the Parousia not occurring as predicted; the political challenge of other authoritative Christian voices (for example, Gnostics) to established orthodox Christianity.

Any authentic discussion of biblical authority must critically examine canonization and include in its query questions such as these:

• Why was it necessary to bury some sacred texts?
• By what criteria were selections made and by whom?
• Who were the threats to orthodox Christian survival?
• What was the nature of the threat (political, religious)?

Canonical criticism enhances the prejudicial or perspectival nature of Scripture and validates the crucial relationship between authority and the confessing community.

Integrative Historical View

"The time is fulfilled, and the kingdom of God is at hand" (Mark 1:15, RSV).

An examination of the Greek identifies the two verbs of this verse in the perfect tense:

πεπλήρωται (from πληρόω—I fulfill)

ἤγγικεν (from ἐγγίζω—I come near, I approach)

This tense suggests an action begun in the past and completed in the present, demonstrating a compatibility with major themes in biblical thought.

Annually during the Passover seder the age-old biblical confession is proclaimed:

"My father was a wandering Aramaean. He went down into Egypt. . . . The Egyptians ill-treated us. . . . But we called on Yahweh. . . . Yahweh heard our voice. . . . He brought us here and gave us this land."

(Deuteronomy 26:5–9, JB)

The story of Yahweh's deliverance of the Israelite people from Egypt is recalled as a particular moment in time, remembered and repeated from generation to generation as an integration of past action, present reality, and future hope.

In a similar way the image of God as Creator is linked to "In the beginning . . ." (Genesis 1:1) and the present tense. Jacob Neusner in *Between Time and Eternity* illustrates:

Redemption is both in the past and in the future. That God not only creates but also redeems is attested by Israel's redemption from Egyptian bondage. The congregation repeats the exultant song of Moses and the people at the Red Sea, not as scholars making a learned allusion, but as participants in the salvation of old and of time to come. Then the people turn to the future and ask that Israel once more be redeemed.

But redemption is not only past and future. When the needy are helped, when the proud are humbled and the lowly are raised . . . redemption is already present. Just as creation is not only in the beginning, but occurs daily, so redemption is not only at the Red Sea, but every day, in humble events. Just as revelation was not at Sinai alone, but takes place whenever people study Torah, whenever God opens their hearts to the commandments, so redemption and creation are daily events.

The great cosmic events of creation in the beginning, redemption at the Red Sea, revelation at Sinai—these are everywhere, everyday at hand . . . Historical events produce a framework into which future events will find a place by which they will be understood.[52]

Biblical and Jewish history embody "history with purpose." As Neusner further expands:

Things did not merely happen to the ancient Israelites. Events were shaped, formed and interpreted by them, made into the raw materials for a renewal of the life of the group . . . History was not merely "one damn thing after another." It had a purpose and was moving somewhere.[53]

This understanding is also compatible to the one expressed by Norman Perrin in *Rediscovering the Teachings of Jesus*. In contrasting Western linear time with the Hebraic notion, he states the following:

We are dealing with a concept in which time is thought of not so much as something which passes from future to past, or past to future, but as opportunity or occasion, as something which is given meaning by that which fills it.[54]

The above serves to illustrate that biblical history is best apprehended within the interrelationship of past, present, and future, viewing them as a continuum rather than as separate entities. This, too, is the historical view for which Gadamer argues.

This chapter demonstrates the usefulness of Gadamer's hermeneutic as a model for ascertaining the nature of biblical authority. The encounter motif, the prejudicial framework, and the historical nature of humanity reflected in Gadamer's theory are also consistencies within biblical thought, thus, suggesting ingredients for an alternative model for the nature of biblical authority.

One foundational premise of Gadamer, namely, the intrinsic historicity of persons, requires further commentary. To be historical beings suggests ineluctable deductions. One major conclusion resides in the changeability of meaning resulting from understanding at a particular point of time. A subsequent development is multiplicity of interpretation depending upon the historicity of writer and interpreter. An illustrative example is provided in the writing of the four Gospels in the New Testament. With different audiences and different controversies from the original viewers of Jesus' words and actions (that is, a different historicity), the authors' material was edited and shaped to effect different purposes. Likewise, each Gospel writer had his own focal point or historicity and, thus, identical events could be interpreted in a variety of ways.

In this mode of thought, meaning is "created" rather than "discovered." That is, the meaning of the text and its application are not separate entities, rather, meaning is derived as melding or fusion occurs, the meeting point of text and interpreter mutually addressing and being addressed by each other.

II. A CLASSICAL DEVELOPMENTAL MODEL FOR CHILDREN

5. Jean Piaget's Developmental Model

The theory of Jean Piaget (1896–1980), the renowned Swiss psychologist, has been used extensively over the years in the training of early childhood educators, counselors of children, public school educators, and, more recently, Christian educators. His theory, often critiqued in terms of method and focus, is uncontested in major conclusions. Any discussion of education, therefore, requires knowledge and application of the Piagetian developmental model.

The purpose of part II is to (a) identify and present Piaget's model of worldview, cognitive development, and moral judgment; (b) critique the model for purposes of clarity and undeveloped factors; and (c) to discuss, in chapter 6, the implications of major conclusions for Christian education. The presentation of Piaget's work is comprehensive. It is presented in depth in order to view the scope and seriousness of Piaget's research and to assess his findings within this perspective. In discussing the implications of major conclusions for Christian education, two major contributors to contemporary Christian religious education are also identified and assessed. One is Thomas H. Groome, teacher of religious education and theology at the Institute of Religious Education and Pastoral Ministry, Boston College, who is recognized for his comprehensive text, *Christian Religious Education*. The other is James Fowler, professor of theology and human development at Chandler School of Theology in Atlanta, a pioneer in the field of faith development. Both use Piagetian theory for their foundational base, and their research is considered necessary for students and teachers of religious education today.

This study will aid the development of a proposal for a biblical model of education with children that gives serious attention to all ingredients: children, education, and Scripture.

The Worldview of the Child

What view of the world do children possess? What is their *weltanschauung*? These are priority questions for understanding the moral judgment and cognitive development of children. Indeed, they are prerequisites for the understanding of any person, culture, or epoch. For example, many biblical passages evoke a response of absurdity when interpreted through a twentieth-century *weltanschauung.* When interpreted through the mythical worldview of prescientific humanity, however, textual understanding is greatly enhanced. An illustration of the biblical worldview is portrayed by Rudolf Bultmann.

The cosmology of the New Testament is essentially mythical in character. The world is viewed as a three-storied structure, with the earth in the center, the heaven above, and the underworld beneath. Heaven is the abode of God and of celestial beings—the angels. The underworld is hell, the place of torment. Even the earth is more than the scene of natural, everyday events of the trivial round and common task. It is the scene of the supernatural activity of God and his angels on the one hand, and of Satan and his demons on the other. These supernatural forces intervene in the course of nature and in all that men think and will and do.

Miracles are by no means rare. Man is not in control of his own life. Evil spirits may take possession of him. Satan may inspire him with evil thoughts. Alternatively, God may inspire his thought and guide his purposes. He may grant him heavenly visions. He may give him the supernatural power of his spirit.[1]

Studied against this background, the temptations of Jesus (Matthew 4:1–11; Mark 1:12–13; Luke 4:1–13), for example, enrich understanding of the person, era, and worldview of Jesus. Without this background, the temptation stories lack meaning.

In relation to this cosmology of the ancient biblical world, Piaget's recurring use of the word "primitive" is noteworthy (for example, primitive realism, primitive association). In its usage by Piaget, "primitive" usually refers to an animistic or mythical belief expressed by children prior to their exposure to the world of logic and science.

Piaget's methodology of observation and clinical examination in ascertaining the worldview of children is characterized by its professional approach, thoroughness, intensity, and scrutiny of results. His findings, as in all other areas of research, are classified around stages of development.

Concerns pertaining to worldview focus around two primary questions: What is "reality" for the child? Who or what causes things to happen? Piaget's entire research around the child's conception of the world evolves around these two foci of reality and causality. His findings are summarized as follows:

Stage I	Stage II	Stage III	Stage IV

(Realism) the notion of thought, i.e., What does it mean to think of something?

Stage I	Stage II	Stage III	Stage IV
We think with our mouths. (5–6 yrs.)	We think with our heads in a material way (related to voice, mouth, brain, neck, etc.). (7–8 yrs.)	We think with our heads; thought is distinguished from things. (after 9–10 yrs.)[2]	

(Nominal Realism) the problem of names (ontological aspect—existence, place, origin).

Stage I	Stage II	Stage III	Stage IV
Names come from things (in the things). We know the names of things by looking at them. The names of things are in the things. (5–6 yrs.)	Names come from persons who made the things (name made with the things). We know the names of things because God told them to us. The names of things are everywhere (becoming apart from the things). (7–8 yrs.)	Names come from other people (persons who thought about the thing). We know the names of things because they were handed down to us by our mothers and fathers. Names are in the voice, then in the head, then in thought itself. Names are immaterial. (after 9, 10 yrs.)[3]	

continues on page 89

Stage I	Stage II	Stage III	Stage IV

The problem of names (logical aspect—intrinsic value).

Stage I	Stage II	Stage III	Stage IV
All names contain the idea of the thing. (up to 10 yrs.)	There is harmony between the name and idea. (10, 11 yrs.)	Name is a sign, contains nothing in itself. (11, 12 yrs.)[4]	

Dreams: What is a dream? Where is the dream? What do you dream with? Why did you dream of . . .?

Stage I	Stage II	Stage III	Stage IV
Dreams come from outside, take place in the room, and remain external to the mind. (5–6 yrs.)	Dreams come from within us but are external. (7–8 yrs.)	Dreams come from within us and are internal; dreams are thoughts, not material images. (after 9, 10 yrs.)[5]	

ANIMISM *(ascribing aliveness and consciousness to objects)*

Purposiveness: Do objects feel anything?

Stage I	Stage II	Stage III	Stage IV
All things are conscious; consciousness is related to activity. (until 6, 7 yrs.)	Moving things are conscious. (6 or 7 to 8 or 9 yrs.)	Things that move of their own accord are conscious. (8 or 9 to 11 or 12 yrs.)	Consciousness is restricted to animals; animism is discarded. (after 11, 12 yrs.)[6]

Concept of Life: Is the (object) alive?

Stage I	Stage II	Stage III	Stage IV
Life is that which has activity or function. (until 6, 7 yrs.)	Life is that which moves. (6–8 yrs.)	Life means spontaneous movement. (8 or 9 to 11, 12 yrs.)	Life is restricted to animals and plants. (11, 12, yrs.)[7]

continues on page 90

Stage I	Stage II	Stage III	Stage IV

Necessity in natural laws, moral necessity or physical determination (Does the sun, moon obey?).

Stage I	Stage II	Stage III
The sun and moon follow us. (5–8 yrs.) Things can't act as they choose; morally obliged to do so for our good. (5–8 yrs.)	The sun does and does not follow. (8–10 yrs.) Things can't act as they choose because of physical constraint; still a large number of objects obey moral laws. (8–10 yrs.)	The sun and moon only appear to follow. (10, 11 yrs.)[8] Things can't act as they choose because of physician determination. (10, 11 yrs.)[9]

Child Artificialism: *"[R]egarding things as the product of human creation rather than in attributing creative activity to the things themselves."*[10] *"[T]he tendency to believe that human beings control the creation and conduct of other beings, which are regarded as being in some degree alive and conscious."*[11]

How are things such as the sun, moon made? What are their origins?

Stage I	Stage II	Stage III
The sun, moon, sky, night, thunder, lightning, etc. are made artificially. (5–8 yrs.)	The origins of the sun, moon, sky, etc. are partly natural (half artificial; half natural). (8–9 yrs.)	The origin of the sun and moon, etc. is completely natural. (10, 11 yrs.)[12]

continues on page 91

Stage I	Stage II	Stage III	Stage IV

How do we get wood, plants, stone, etc.?

Stage I	Stage II	Stage III	Stage IV
(Same as above) integral artificialism.	(Same as above) mixture of artificialism and natural explanation.	(Same as above) natural explanation.[13]	

Summary—The "Weltanschauung" of the Child

From the foregoing, Piaget assesses the child's conception of the world as that of a realist; that is, subject is indistinguishable from its object ("to think is to deal with words").[14] Within this frame of reference, animism and artificialism enable the child to comprehend the functioning of her or his world. The world is described in the possessive of "her or his" since the child identifies with a self-centered view of the world—"self-centered," not as synonymous with "selfish" but as a world which centers around herself or himself. Piaget describes the naturalness of this perspective:

From the outset of his conscious life, the child is immediately dependent on his parents' activity for food, comfort, shelter and clothing which are all organized for him in accordance with his requirements. The most natural idea for him . . . is that all nature centres around him and has been organized by his parents or by humans beings in general.[15]

As previously noted, Piaget views children in stages of development, corresponding with ages of development. Realism, animism, and artificialism, thus, move through various phases of decline during childhood. For example, the phases of realism are categorized as follows:

1. Absolute realism: instruments of thought and object are indistinguishable.
2. Immediate realism: instruments of thought are distinguishable from objects but are situated in the object.
3. Mediate realism: instruments of thought are located both within the object and outside of it—they are semidistinguishable.
4. Subjectivism or relativism: instruments of thought are distinguishable from things and are located within themselves.[16]

Likewise, four phases are identified for artificialism:

1. Diffuse artificialism: nature is either controlled by human beings or focuses around them.[17]
2. Mythological artificialism: nature has mythical origins.[18]
3. Technical artificialism: the control of human beings over nature is complemented by laws of nature.[19]
4. Immanent artificialism: "Nature inherits the attributes of man and manufactures in the style of the craftsman or artist."[20]

The phases of animism are closely related to those of artificialism.

The religious development of the child is inseparable from the above noted stages. Piaget's observation from interviewing children was that God was the "last resort" in their responses; that is, God entered the conversation when all other possible solutions were exhausted. In particular, "the religious instruction imparted to children between the ages of four and seven often appears as something foreign to the child's natural thought."[21]

In this regard, Piaget affirms the thesis, "according to which the child spontaneously attributes to his parents the perfections and attributes which he will later transfer to God if his religious education gives him the opportunity. . . . In short, God is either a man like other men, or else the child is always romancing when he speaks of him, in the same way that he speaks of Father Christmas and the fairies."[22]

Piaget's phrase to summarize the child's conception of the world is "ontological egocentricity";[23] that is, reality is viewed within the framework of humanity as the center of the universe. All other questions, thoughts, and assertions are considered within this "syncretic schema."

The Cognitive Development of the Child

An understanding of intellectual development in children is pivotal since all other development (for example, moral judgment, behavior) stems from it. Here Piaget identifies three stages and corresponding ages:

Stage I. Sensorimotor intelligence (0–2 years).

Stage II. Preparation and organization of concrete operations of categories, relations, and numbers (2–11 years).

Stage III. Formal operations (11 or 12–13 or 14 years.)[24]

Each of these stages is subdivided to demonstrate the progression of development. For example, within the period of sensorimotor intelligence are six substages:

1. *Reflex exercises* (up to 1 month):[25] The two reflex actions of greater importance for future development are those of sucking and hand movements. Through the functional exercise of sucking, a newborn quickly discovers the nipple, resulting in "a

generalizing assimilation"[26] (sucking on nothing between meals or sucking new objects) and "a recognition assimilation (distinguishing the nipple from other objects)."[27] Thus, within the first month after birth, the origins of intelligence are detected.

2. *First habits* (1–4½ months):[28] Thumb-sucking serves as a prime example during this stage—an action initiated by the infant, experienced as satisfying, and repeated to re-live that experience. This is described as a "primary circular reaction" and "involves an action on the part of the infant which fortuitously leads to an event which has value for him and which is centered around his own body. The infant then learns to repeat the behavior in order to reinstate the event. The culmination of the process is an organized scheme."[29]

3. *Coordination of vision and prehension* (4½–8 or 9 months):[30] Here begins "secondary circular reactions,"[31] for attention is now directed towards the environment where objects are grasped and manipulated. Again, when satisfying results are obtained, the behavior is repeated in the hope of accomplishing the same result. Piaget identifies this substage as the "threshold of intelligence."[32]

4. *Coordination of the secondary schemes* (8 or 9–11 or 12 months):[33] More intentional goals are identified here and, thus, more identifiable intelligence—an obvious example in this substage being an infant attempting to obtain an object out of reach. The criteria used to justify this intentionality of goal, classified as intelligence, are as follows:

(a) The infant has the goal in mind from the beginning and does not discover it accidentally as was the case in stage 3;

(b) An obstacle arises which prevents direct attainment of the goal and necessitates some kind of indirect approach;

(c) To overcome the obstacle, he employs a scheme (means) which is different from that employed in the case of the goal (ends).[34]

5. *Differentiation of schemes of action by tertiary circular reaction* (11 or 12–18 months):[35] Through exploration and experimentation, new alternatives to achieve goals are discovered in this period. Synonymous with new alternatives is the acquisition of new skills. Again, using the example of an object out of reach, a child discovers that several alternatives are available: using a stick, pulling the blanket, etc.[36]

6. *Beginning of the interiorization of the schemes and solution of a few problems with action stopping and sudden understanding* (18–24 months):[37] This stage, marking the completion of sensorimotor intelligence, is summarized as "insight."[38] Piaget's illustration of this stage is a child with a partially opened matchbox with a thimble inside. A stage 5 response is initially that of groping, then upon failure the child ceases the action, pauses to consider the situation, and opens the box by slipping his fingers into the open space. While examining the situation, the child is observed as opening and closing his mouth or hand.[39]

Stage I is the period of development prior to language.

In a comparable manner, stage II has two subdivisions, which are also subdivided:

1. *The subperiod of preoperatory representations* (2 years to 7 or 8 years):[40]
   a. Symbolic function (2 years to 3½ or 4 years):

Through the use of symbolism (language, visual images, symbolic play or imagination), the child moves to an advanced level of development enabling the child to commence articulation, reasoning, and the maturation process towards emotional stability. "Symbolic function" identifies the child's ability "to make something—a mental symbol, a word, or an object—stand for or represent something else which is not present."[41]

b. Representative organizations founded either on static configurations or on assimilation to the action itself (4 years to 5½ years):[42] In this period the child is able to reproduce static images of sights previously experienced.[43]

c. Articulated representative regulations (5½ years to 7 or 8 years):[44] This is the transitional phase between nonconservation and conservation, that is, the ability to identify equivalence of objects or substances when rearrangement has occurred. For example, conservation of substance is evidenced at this time but not that of weight or volume.[45] It is also the transitional period between static images and kinetic (changes in position) and transformational images (changes in shape or form).

A general characteristic of this whole subperiod is "centration"—the ability to focus on limited information or parts of a situation rather than the integrated whole.[46]

2. *The subperiod of concrete operations* (7 or 8 years to 11 or 12 years):[47] "Concrete" is a key word in this phase, defining operations relating directly to objects rather than articulated hypotheses.[48] In contrast to the "centration" of the preoperational child, "decentration"[49]—the ability to focus on several aspects of a situation or prob-

lem at once—occurs. Thus, conservation of number occurs as the child is now able to coordinate length and density. Likewise, conservation of substance, weight, and volume occur.[50] Children are also capable of representation of kinetic and transformational images and reversibility of mental operations.

3. *The period of formal operations* (11 or 12 years to 13 or 14 years):[51] Many rapid and varied transformations occur during this stage.

- Combinative operations (combinations, permutations, etc.) enabling the child to create "sets of parts" and network structures
- Appearance of proportions (spatial proportions, metrical speeds, probabilities, etc.)
- Reasoning and self-representation
- Logic of propositions—the ability to solve problems of verbally stated hypotheses, in contrast to concrete operations[52]

Abstract thought and complex problem reasoning are the chief characteristics of the above, enabling the child to consider solutions and alternate solutions to problems and, thus, flexibility of thought.

The Moral Judgment of the Child

Closely related to cognitive development, in Piaget's theory, is moral development. Moral development or judgment is differentiated from moral rules, for the latter are imposed upon children by adults. Moral judgment, on the other hand, is developmental with several stages, influenced by environment but not solely dependent upon it.

Piaget agrees with Kant and Durkheim that "all morality consists of rules, and the essence of all morality is to be sought for in the respect which the individual acquires for these rules."[53] He, thus, observes and examines children in the game of marbles. As a result of this procedure, Piaget concluded that children, at various ages, move through four successive stages in the game:

1. An individualistic stage (to 2 years): Children handle marbles according to personal desire and acquired motor habits.
2. An egocentric stage (2–5 years): Through imitation a child attempts to follow the observed rules of the game but is unaware of the game's competitive nature. A child may continue to play by himself or herself or may seek a partner; in either instance the focus is upon self.
3. Stage of incipient cooperation (between 7 and 8 to 11 years): The focus is now on competition and winning with observance of rules as the priority.
4. Stage of codification of rules (between 11 and 12 years): Minute details of the game are emphasized and acceptance of mutually consented rules is imperative; that is, rules may be changed beforehand, but once agreed upon, adherence to the rules is essential.[54]

From stage 2, consciousness of rules is common but with different characteristics: noncoercive character in stage 2; its sacred character in stage 3; and the mutually consented aspect of rules in stage 4.[55] Children move from submission to rules to rules by consensus.

In his moral judgment research, Piaget also used the clinical examination method, inviting children to resolve stories containing a moral dilemma. For example:

A child is looking at a picture book belonging to his father. Instead of being careful, he makes spots on several of the pages. What shall the father do?

1. The child will not go to the cinema that evening.
2. The father will not lend him the book any more.
3. The child often lends his stamp album to his father; the father will not take care of it as he has always done up to then.

Other stories are more open-ended with no choices given. In some instances, contrasting stories were related to the question, "Which of the two was the naughtiest and why?" For example:

A. A little boy who is called John is in his room. He is called to dinner. He goes into the dining room. But behind the door there was a chair, and on the chair there was a tray with fifteen cups on it. John couldn't have known that there was all this behind the door. He goes in, the door knocks against the tray, bang go the fifteen cups, and they all get broken!

B. Once there was a little boy whose name was Henry. One day when his mother was out he tried to get some jam out of the cupboard. He climbed up on to a chair and stretched out his arm. But the jam was too high up and he couldn't reach it and have any. But while he was trying to get it he knocked over a cup. The cup fell down and broke.[56]

A common characteristic of all stories is the "What do you think?" emphasis. Findings demonstrated that children moved from declaring that punishment equals the misdemeanor, to considering motives in determining punishment, to entertaining the idea that a mistake made with the intent of helping requires no punishment and, in fact, punishment would be an act of injustice.

Through this extensive research, three stages of moral development are identified:

Stage I. *A moral constraint or pre-moral stage:*[57] Here the child obeys because it is the command of a respected adult—the genesis of

moral obligation. For example, "the obligation to speak the truth, not to steal, etc. are
all so many duties which the child feels very
deeply, although they do not emanate from
his mind. They are commands coming from
the adult and accepted by the child."[58] This
stage is also a preparatory period for future
cooperation.

Stage II. *The heteronomy stage (ages 4– 8):*[59] Here
literal obedience to the law is all important.
Heteronomy and moral realism are interre-
lated, the latter being a structure "according
to which obligations and values are determined by the law or the order itself, inde-
pendent of intentions and relationships."[60]
Objective responsibility is also characteristic of this stage; that is, acts are evaluated in
terms of disobedience to the law without regard for intent or motive.[60]

Stage III. *The autonomy stage (8– 12 years):*[62] Reciprocity or mutual respect is the key ingredient in this stage. Justice is dominant with
intent or motive rather than law the determining factors. The influence of interper-
sonal relationships in moral development is
most vividly demonstrated in this stage.

Piaget summarizes:

Now, apart from our relations to other people, there can be
no moral necessity. The individual as such knows only an-
omy and not autonomy. Conversely, any relation with other
persons, in which unilateral respect takes place, leads to
heteronomy. Autonomy therefore appears only with reciprocity, when mutual respect is strong enough to make the

individual feel within the desire to treat others as he himself would wish to be treated.[63]

Summary

From the above, the interrelatedness of a child's *weltanschauung*, cognitive development, and moral judgment are evident, with cognitive development as the controlling factor. Because of "centration," a child of five years is unable to assess intent and motive in determining disobedience to the law. In a similar way, the ability to reason abstractly in stage III of cognitive development enables the child to discard animism and artificialism. The relationships are diagrammed as shown in illustration 5.

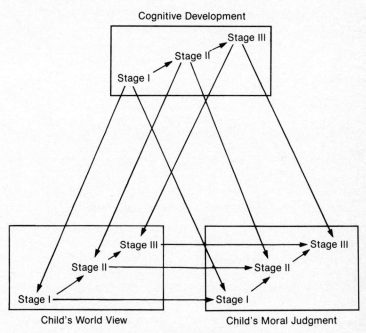

5. Piaget's Developmental Model

A Critical Examination

I have chosen to comment on Piaget's model by identifying concepts requiring further clarification and/or research.

Nature/Nurture Paradox

Environmental versus hereditary influences require further clarity in Piaget's theory. Piaget ignores this concern as nonsensical. Of prime importance are the stages of development:

There certainly is such a thing as a sensorimotor intelligence, but it is very difficult to specify the exact moment when it appears. Actually, the question makes no sense, for the answer always depends upon an arbitrary choice of criterion. What one actually finds is a remarkably smooth succession of stages, each marking a new advance, until the moment when the acquired behavior presents characteristics that one or another psychologist recognizes as those of "intelligence."[64]

To validate his theory, however, more than an irrelevant response to these crucial factors is required. In reality, Piaget attributes considerable emphasis to the activity, rather than the passivity, of the child at birth towards the environment through the illustration of the sucking reflex. Peter Berger reconciles the nature/nurture paradox in recognizing the innate dialectic character of this social phenomenon; persons are both creators and products of society or environment.

Society is a dialectic phenomenon in that it is a human product. . . . Society is a product of man. . . . Yet . . . man is a product of society. Every individual biography is an episode within the history of society, which both precedes and survives it. . . . It is within society . . . that the individual becomes a person.[65]

Piaget's recorded research analysis affirms support of Berger's sociological theory in that he acknowledges the innateness of intelligence and the essential role of education in enabling children to progress through the various stages of development.

Age Limitations

The rigidity of age associated with the various stages of development (especially moral development) also requires reassessment. A casual observation of society demonstrates that many adults have not achieved the autonomous stage of supposedly 8 to 12-year-olds (for example, the stress upon retributive justice in society). Lawrence Kohlberg, a supporter of Piagetian theory, discovered that only 10 percent of adults have reached this stage.[66]

This Way Only!

Inherent in the concept of stages in both Kohlberg and Piaget is an "invariant sequence," making it impossible to regress, except under extreme conditions.[67] Such a theory is incompatible with life experiences where individuals fluctuate in their moral judgment.

Boys Only, Please

Piaget's constituency for research was chiefly boys. Surprisingly, Kohlberg, the "Piaget" of America, worked with only boys in his original sampling.[68] This raises serious questions because of the conditioning and bias of traditional society on *vive la difference* between female and male. Would similar findings result if the group were all female or mixed? Two differing opinions (at least) respond to this query. Dr. David Elkind, professor of psychology at the University of Rochester, researched and tested Piaget's theory by interviewing children of both genders. His findings were similar to those of Piaget.[69]

Carol Gilligan, a Harvard colleague of Kohlberg, suggests that in terms of moral reasoning, Kohlberg's assessment measures are sexually biased (a result of males interviewing males). Her data for this postulation are derived from interviews with women in abortion consultations. The women tended to be active participants with personal investment in the issue rather than objective analysts. One might applaud this approach of moral decision making and, in fairness to the male of the species, surmise that men involved in moral decision making around capital punishment, when the murderers are their sons, might also portray visible traits of personal investment. On Kohlberg's measurement scales, however, "subjective attachment . . . this central organizing impulse of women was scored as a weakness."[70] More research is obviously required in this area with a mixed constituency of females and males.

Moral Judgment vs. Moral Action

Piaget's presuppositions that moral judgment results in moral action and that moral judgment is a prerequisite for moral action are debatable. Moral judgment is based on cognitive reasoning, whereas moral action demands extra ingredients related to conviction, fullness of time, conscience, etc. For example, as a global village we have discerned the injustice of unequal distribution of the world's goods without remedying the situation. The United States of America knowingly treated its black people unjustly, but it took a fatigued Rosa Parks at the end of a long, tiring day to refuse to move to the rear of the bus to end one aspect of gross injustice among her people. The corollary also holds true. Children and adults alike often act in moral ways without the act of discernment or articulation.

Relationship to Other Disciplines

Piaget's methodology and thesis are formulated within the framework of psychological developmentalism, the contemporary dominant school pertaining to educational theory and religious education. Other approaches provide alternative perspectives, not necessarily to counter but to parallel that of Piaget, broadening one's perspective on childhood capabilities.

For example, using an anthropological approach, Edward Robinson in *The Original Vision* claims that children are capable of and, indeed, experience profound religious moments that have a permanent influence on their lives.

Robinson's thesis is derived from interviews with approximately 500 adults who attest to pivotal and vivid religious childhood experiences.[71] Throughout the interviews are eye-catching statements:

I had my first religious experience when I was about six.[72]

The most profound experience of my life came to me when I was very young—between four and five years old.[73]

As a child (not younger than 6, not older than 8) I had an experience which nowadays I consider as kindred, if not identical, with those experiences related by Wordsworth in the Prelude, Bk. 1, lines 379–400.[74]

In making this claim for religious experience in childhood, indeed, for "religious experience as a central feature of human life,"[75] Robinson's definition of the "religious" is informed by the imagination, the arts, affections, mystery, wonder, and awe as opposed to instructional, institutional religion and theology. Since what one is capable of articulating cognitively does not limit what one is capable of knowing experientially, this aspect of cognitive development in Piaget's theory can be challenged. Cognitive religious instruction may be foreign to the natural thought of children, while religious experience may be intrinsic to it.

Also, unlike Piaget, Robinson views childhood as an aspect of personhood, a necessity for wholeness of being, as opposed to the Piagetian view of childhood as a developmental stage along the road to adult maturity.[76]

Other deficiencies in research are recognized by Piaget, notably the highly subjective nature of the research and, thus, the number of variables to be considered (for example: mood and mind set of practitioners, biases, context, geography, culture, lifestyle, language). Remarkably, however, there is a recognized cross-cultural generality in Piaget's findings. That is, tested research in England, the United States, Canada, Israel, India, and other countries produced similar findings.[77]

The strength of Piaget's model is demonstrated by this consensus among developmental theorists in diverse cultures and countries. His attention to the cognitive development, moral judgment, and worldview of children illustrates the integrative approach of his research. In critically examining this work, some limitations were identified, especially in the areas of the religious nature of children and the limited constituency of boys. These new ingredients serve to amplify Piaget's contribution to the nature of childhood. The acknowledgment of regression as well as progression in developmental theory and greater attention to the nature/nurture controversy would have enhanced his theory. Rather than fallacies in argument, however, these are areas for further clarification.

I would conclude, therefore, that the work of Jean Piaget is a serious and necessary ingredient in any discussion of education, including education in a Christian context. The next chapter, then, examines the implications of Piaget's developmental theory for Christian education, furthering the goal of establishing an adequate biblical model in education with children.

6. Implications for Christian Education

Several assumptions about children, learning, knowledge, and religion are deduced from Piaget's developmental model and a critical examination of it.

Assumptions about Children
- Children develop physically, psychologically (including moral discernment), and intellectually through interconnected, progressive stages.
- Children are innately curious creatures and initiate much of their own learning.
- Children learn at their own unique rate within the various developmental stages.
- Children's intelligence is observed from birth—the origins of intelligence during the first month and the "threshold of intelligence" from 4½–9 months.

Assumptions about Learning
- Children learn through exploration and experimentation in order to achieve their own goals.
- Much of children's learning is spontaneous, that is, without an adult-imposed, structured learning environment.
- Children learn through play and demonstrate their developmental characteristics through it.
- Children learn initially by concrete operations through actions and interaction, and reflection upon the environment. They need to observe, touch, and manipulate objects for learning.

- Emphasis in learning is on the person rather than on the subject.
- In learning, attention is required in both affective and cognitive domains (for example, feelings and content are both important).
- The task of education is to enable children to progress through the various stages of development.
- The learnings from primary socialization (for example, fear, trust, belonging, rejection, etc.) form an entrenched "syncretic schema" from early childhood.
- Learning occurs within a societal framework; society both informs learning and is informed by it.

Assumptions about Knowledge

- Children possess a worldview, a *weltanschauung,* unique to their development; this *weltanschauung,* prior to the stage of abstract reasoning (approximately 12 years), is largely animistic, artificial, and mythical.
- Children's view of the world is categorized as realistic and egocentric; that is, subject is indistinguishable from object and "world" is that which centers around them.
- Knowledge is characterized in stage II of development (2–8 years) by "centration," the ability to focus on limited information or parts of a situation rather than the integrated whole.
- Knowledge is characterized in stage III of development (7 or 8–11, 12 years) by "decentration," the ability to focus on several aspects of a situation or problem.

Assumptions about Religion

- Children up to the age of 7 do not naturally speak of God; religious statements are usually those imposed from the adult world and are not compatible with their natural thought.
- In their development, children transfer their image of

parental divinity to that of God; God becomes the Supreme Parent.

- During the early stage of development, God and Jesus are treated in a similar way as Santa Claus, fairies, etc.
- Children are capable of deep religious experiences that influence their lives in profound ways; the articulated abstraction of these experiences usually occurs much later.

Within these assumptions, those concerning knowledge comprise the theoretical frame of reference from which all other assumptions flow. That is, an understanding of knowledge is essential for any significant discussions regarding the methodology and content of education.

Considerations for Christian Education

The seriousness of the Christian religious education enterprise is tempered by the awareness of the novelty of the Sunday school movement (the organization synonymous with Christian education for Protestant churches), founded in England by Robert Raikes in 1780.[1] This, of course, means that for approximately seventeen hundred years the tenets of the faith were sufficiently transmitted to maintain Christian religious institutions and build a society claiming its foundational base as the Judaeo-Christian heritage. Another implication is the freedom to explore alternative models for Christian education in the church today, recognizing that no socially constructed model is sacred.

Implications

According to the Piagetian developmental model, abstract concepts are not appropriate instruction until children attain stage III or IV in their development. This would suggest that for religion to have a "staying power" rather than be discarded as a fairy tale, abstract religious concepts (for example, God as Creator) are inappropriate at any early stage. The rationale for this assessment is linked to Piaget's findings that during the early stages of development God and Jesus are comprehended in a similar manner as Santa Claus, fairies, etc. As children develop, moving from mythological artificialism to technical and immanent artificialism, they discard Santa Claus and fairies and later recognize them as belonging to the world of fantasy, legend, etc. That is, they no longer become powerful forces in children's lives. It is reasonable to assume, then, that religious concepts would be treated by children in a similar manner. Another inadequacy is the possible re-creation for children of the "God of the gaps" theory of the eighteenth century; that is, God becomes the explanation of that which is scientifically unexplainable. As more scientific knowledge is discovered, the gap narrows until God is obliterated. When children reach the latter part of stage III in development, they commence to apprehend the literary nature of Scripture, noting the difference between poetry, legend, history, myth, etc. and the various ways biblical people comprehended God, Jesus, the Church, the world, etc.

This is a paradoxical concern, however. The research of Edward Robinson in *The Original Vision* portrays children as capable of profound religious insight. Those involved with children know that children, indeed very young children of ages 3 and 4, are often obsessed with questions "why," suggesting a desire to know cause and effect. This at least implies abstract thought.

Neither of the above positions implies, however, that religious activity or stories of the faith are censored for younger children. What is does imply is that these activities are enacted within the context of community.

Through the primary use of religious symbol and metaphor, visually and dramatically represented, baptism and communion become two pivotal Christian celebrations for involvement in symbolic religious community. In *Religious Education Development,* Gabriel Moran defines metaphor as "statement or implied statements that are literally false but which awaken the imagination to the mystery of things." He affirms metaphor as "the process by which language keeps transcending itself" and asserts "Religious development . . . occurs by means of metaphors that are based on imagination, nourished in community, and rooted in tradition."[2] Religious language of metaphor and symbol is one way to address the concern of abstract concepts with children; these can be apprehended if represented in concrete form.

Acknowledging the permanency of primary socialization and the necessity of secondary socialization in development, the nuclear family and the church community become essential ingredients for the religious development of children. As children observe that respected adults, who uphold scientific worldviews, are involved in worship and education as regular and significant expressions in their lives, these children begin to view religion as natural for particular groupings of people, rather than something "children do." That is, children observe that, while adults have discarded Santa Claus and fairy tales, religious expression is an intentional part of adult life. For example, a parent or teacher may teach children to pray (for example: close your eyes, fold your hands, and repeat after me, "Now I lay me down to sleep . . ."), and children will usually acquiesce. Prayer, however, will hold more significance and permanence if experienced as a family activity, a church activity, and a natural topic for discussion and debate in both environments. The "naming" of activity (that is, abstract concepts) is acquired as children query the rationale, which would probably emerge earlier than stage III or IV in a communal context. In this context, adults are provided with the opportunity to affirm their convictions and share their own questions with children, acknowledging that they, too, are growing in their understanding of the world from a religious viewpoint.

Another key concept, derived from the foregoing discussion of Piaget, is that the essential starting point in any educational endeavor is the life-experience of children. This concept is also a reiteration of John Dewey (1859–1952), the influential educational theorist and philosopher of the early 1900s: "[E]ducation in order to accomplish its ends both for the individual learner and for society must be based upon experience—which is always the actual life-experience of some individual."[3]

Lest one fear inadequate or inappropriate learning in this approach, it is necessary to reflect on the monumental learnings during the first five years of life, largely initiated by the child's sense of curiosity toward the environment without the aid of structured learning environments. In fact, this learning is often impeded by the institutional environment imposed thereafter. In relation to Christian education it is difficult to suggest a subject or theme crucial for comprehension at a given age. Again, to cite Dewey:

It is no reflection on the nutritive quality of beefsteak that it is not fed to infants. It is not an invidious reflection upon trigonometry that we do not teach it in the first or fifth grade of school. It is not the subject per se that is educative or that is conducive to growth. There is no subject that is in and of itself, or without regard to the stage of growth attained by the learner, such that inherent educational value can be attributed to it.[4]

Christians err in their overzealous desire to ensure that children are verbally exposed to every aspect of the faith, regardless of whether anyone is asking the question or, indeed, is interested in pursuing it. This enthusiasm often counters our knowledge of child development and accomplishes the opposite of what we intend; that is, children become bored, frustrated, or apathetic to Christian education and/or institutionalized Christian expression.

Discussion, thus far, indicates at least three implications for Christian religious education:

1. There is a need for more "intergenerational" home and church Christian education activities, including corporate worship.
2. Any Christian education program is strengthened by adult, as well as children's, groups.
3. The starting point in Christian education is the life experience of the individual.

Theoretically, this discussion finds congruency in the assumptions about learning and knowledge derived from Piaget (activity is crucial and knowledge emerges from it) and the biblical view of "knowing." Thomas Groome summarizes the latter as follows:

In the biblical understanding . . . people come to know the Lord in the midst of historical experience, by reflecting on the activity of God there, by entering a relationship with God and God's people, and by their lived response to that relationship. But their knowing is informed by and interpreted through the Story that has arisen from the previous "knowing" of God's people, and is shaped by the hopes they have in God's promise for their future. From a biblical perspective, then, Christian religious education should be grounded in a relational/experiential/reflective way of knowing that is informed by the Story of faith from Christians before us, and by the Vision toward which that Story points.[5]

Christian education instruction is analogous to teaching children their ancestral family. Initially, children experience key members through visits, telephone calls, and/or letters, initiated by adults. Later, through question or discussion they learn the meaning of names, "Aunt Mary" (father's sister) or "Grandpa" (mother's father). During this time they become conscious of stories about relatives living and dead (the emigration from another country, the pioneering, the tragedies, the jokes, etc.) and eventually become conscious that these people and stories have molded the lives of their parents and are shaping their lives. Some stories are exaggerated (for example, an extraordinary tale that becomes embellished with each generation to illustrate the obstinacy of great-great-grandma); some are exciting; some are boring; all are a part of one's ancestral story. Some stories are not related to children until they are old enough to understand motive and circumstances; other are freely narrated before they fully comprehend the words. Later, children become aware that other families have their own stories. Ideally, they learn that their "family tree" story is not better than another's but different, and, because it is different, ritual activity and behavior may differ or be simply based on different stories. Children could encounter the Judaeo-Christian story through a similar mode.

Relationship with Other Theories

Drawing upon theorists in the fields of education, societal theory, biblical scholarship, and theology, Thomas Groome then uses his own scholarship and experience and formulates the "praxis" model of education as the one most compatible with these concerns for Christian education, claiming that it is consistent with the Piagetian and biblical perspective.[6]

A "praxis" model was advocated initially by Paulo Freire in *Pedagogy of the Oppressed* as the mode of achieving liberation by the oppressed from their oppressors. In his book, Freire, identifies a second stage in which the "praxis" model becomes "a pedagogy of all men in the process of permanent liberation."[7] Opposed to the traditional "banking"[8] method of education that is "antidialogical" and "non-communicative"[9] and results in the dichotomy of oppressor and oppressed, Freire claims the "praxis" method as dialogical and communicative (ingredients of humanization) and results in freedom from oppression for both oppressor and oppressed. In defining praxis, Freire analyses the "essence of dialogue" as "the Word." The Word, in turn, has "two dimensions, reflection and action, in such radical interaction that if one is sacrificed—even in part—the other immediately suffers." He states: There is no true word that is not at the same time a praxis. Thus, to speak a true word is to transform the world."[10]

The praxis model of education, then, is not practice versus theory; it is theory and practice, reflection and action, and results in the transformation of the world.[11]

The ambiguity in the above explanation is identified, by Groome, as one inadequacy in Freire's treatise. Another inadequacy, cited by him, is the lack of attention to the past.[12] Argues Groome, "If the past is forgotten and left unreclaimed, it will determine and control our present. If it is critically appropriated, it can be emancipatory."[13] Dewey cites a similar problem while advocating the theory of experience.

[A]ny theory and set of practices is dogmatic which is not based upon critical examination of its own underlying principles . . . .

[W]e have the problem of discovering the connection which actually exists within experience between the achievements of the past and the issues of the present. We have the problem of ascertaining how acquaintance with the past may be translated into a potent instrumentality for dealing effectively with the future . . . .

How shall the young become acquainted with the past in such a way that the acquaintance is a potent agent in appreciation of the living present?[14]

The Shared-Praxis Model

Desirous, then, of maintaining the "story of the faith community" (past and present) in a dialogical context, Groome proposes his definition of Christian religious education by "shared praxis" as "a group of Christians sharing in dialogue their critical reflection on present action in light of the Christian story and its Vision toward the end of lived Christian faith."[15] Groome identifies five movements in the accomplishment of this purpose:

1. The participants are invited to name their own activity concerning the topic for attention (present action).

2. They are invited to reflect on why they do what they do, and what the likely or intended consequences of their actions are (critical reflection).

3. The educator makes present to the group the Christian community Story concerning the topic at hand and the faith response it invites (story and its vision).

4. Participants are invited to appropriate the Story to their lives in a dialectic between Story and stories.

5. There is an opportunity to choose a personal faith response for the future (dialectic between Vision and visions).[16]

Groome contends that, in light of the Piaget developmental model, children are capable of this approach to education (in a limited way) at approximately seven years of age, when they begin to think concretely.[17] Groome's "shared praxis" proposal is both comprehensive and sound, philosophically, theologically, and educationally. In critique, there are two areas of inadequacy.

The first is the lack of attention given to critical examination of the Christian community Story. While asserting that the presenter of such material be "well-informed, relying upon authentic scholarship and church teaching,"[18] there is no awareness that this material in itself requires critical reflection initially by the presenter(s) followed by the participants. For Groome, critical reflection of the Story enters the process with a question such as, How does this Story related to my(our) story? Indeed, critical examination may determine that the particular aspect of the Story to be presented has minimal or no relationship to the contemporary stories under discussion. The encounter motif identified in Gadamer's hermeneutic is a corrective to this inadequacy.

Second, Groome neglects one prime factor in the process, that of adult education. A radical change is essential in traditional concepts of both education and faith for the feasibility of this model. If Christian educators (for example, parents, teachers, leaders) are to adopt a "shared praxis" approach and abandon the "banking" method of education, retraining and continuous education are mandatory. If Christian educators are to view faith as developmental rather than as a changeless entity, a radical shift in emphasis and behavior is required. Here James Fowler and his faith development theory contribute useful insights to complement Groome's model. Fowler is widely recognized for this pioneer work, and any serious study in the area of religious education demands consideration of his work.

Faith Development

Traditionally, we conceive of faith as a subject or object. But, Fowler contends, "faith is not a noun but a verb."[19] A more accurate rendition for Fowler would be to acknowledge that faith is both noun and verb. His purpose, however, was to provide a corrective to the conventional equating of faith as ideological belief systems and appropriate religious activities. Both he and Groome maintain that "faith is a lifelong developmental process involving the total person."[20] It is around this premise that Fowler, through survey and research, identifies seven stages of faith development. These stages, too, rely upon Piaget for their foundational base.

In capsule form these stages are defined as follows:

Undifferentiated Faith: This is called a pre-stage where the foundation for faith is laid (for example: trust, courage, hope, and love or their opposites).

Intuitive-Projective Faith: This is the stage of children from 3 to 7, prior to concrete operational thinking. The faith of parents as apprehended by children, embellished with fantasy, imagination, artificial thinking, etc., is the main characteristic.

Mythic-Literal Faith: Story becomes the major means of appropriation, with one dimensional, literal interpretation as a way of finding meaning in life. Faith as handed down is the "owned" faith. This stage is primarily that of the 7 to 11 year old.

Synthetic-Conventional Faith: Faith now extends beyond the family to the "peer" group, which is the major determinative factor in values and faith. It is the "conformist" stage of faith; what significant others hold as the "norm" is crucial.

Individuative-Reflective Faith: Here faith is debated, questioned, rejected as persons seek for their own identity, including a faith of their own. What others think is no longer a major consideration and persons are ready to assume responsibility for themselves.

Conjunctive Faith: Here we find the integration and reconciliation of much that was unresolved in the previous stages. The past is reclaimed in a new way and people of other races, creeds, and classes are viewed as an enrichment to life.

Through experience, persons in this stage (to use Fowler's words), "alive to paradox and the truth in apparent contradictions," can reconcile opposites in an empowering way.

Universalizing Faith: This is the stage of faith that many envy and few obtain. In this stage are persons who view life and faith beyond themselves, have a deep insight into the ultimate meaning of life and live it. Classic personages like Gandhi, Martin Luther King, Jr., and Mother Teresa are illustrations of this stage. To quote Fowler, such persons are "incarnators and actualizers of the Spirit of an inclusive and fulfilled human community."[21]

These stages initially appear as ages with "Synthetic-Conventional Faith" occurring during adolescence and "Conjunctive Faith" emerging in the middle years. Fowler's research, however, indicates that some adults demonstrated characteristics of the "Mythic-Literal Faith" of stage 2, many were in stage 3 (Synthetic-Conventional Faith), many did not reach stage 4 (Individuative-Reflective Faith), for a significant number of adults, stage 4, was not evident until the midthirties or forties.[22] In elaborating on the "Synthetic-Conventional faith" of stage 3, he states

Many critics of religion and religious institutions assume, mistakenly, that to be religious in an institution necessarily means to be Synthetic-Conventional . . . This mistake by critics is understandable. Much of church and synagogue life in this country can be accurately described as dominantly Synthetic-Conventional.[23]

In conclusion, then, the Christian church has a macroscopic task in developing a Christian religious education program for children that is faithful to (a) child development, (b) Scripture, and (c) an authentic education.

Adult education requires special attention. Resources would be person-centered, providing opportunity for critical reflection with integrated liaison between home and the corporate faith community. Adults and children would normally worship and learn together.

The next task is one of synthesis. Part I of this book produced significant findings concerning biblical authority, while part II provided theoretical background on child development as represented by Jean Piaget, examined it critically, and discussed in depth its implications for Christian education. Two Piagetian supporters and contributors to Christian education theory and practice, Thomas H. Groome and James Fowler, were also acknowledged and the unresolved task of an authentic biblical model identified with further ingredients added.

Now a synthesis must occur between biblical authority and interpretation, children and education. This is the central focus of part III. In that section, findings to date will be identified and an alternative model of biblical education with children proposed.

III. WHAT DOES THIS ALL MEAN?

7. A New Encounter Model of Biblical Authority

In this book, several dimensions of biblical authority have been explored in the search for an acceptable position and an authentic model of biblical education with children. The varied parts are complex for valid reasons. The ingredients of Scripture, children, and education demanded an interdisciplinary approach, employing primarily those of philosophy, theology, and education. To identify and define the problem, the social reality of Scripture as represented through a major denomination was portrayed and analysed. To do justice to the thesis, contemporary and historical resources were utilized. The ingredients of children and education called for serious consideration of child development theory and its implications for Christian education.

To recount the story thus far, the book began with a presentation and critical examination of biblical authority as represented by The United Church of Canada through its official doctrinal statements and the curricula it presently recommends. Three biblical models—identified as the models of (a) ultimate authority, (b) Christocentric, and (c) contextual—were illustrated. Each model was critically examined and its inadequacies demonstrated. Each model was to be also observed incompatible with the others.

For a classical, historical, and theological perspective,

the hermeneutic of Johann August Ernesti, undergirding the ultimate authority model, was examined. While Ernesti's contribution to the hermeneutical endeavour was recognized, there were deficiencies in his biblical hermeneutic, as identified in chapter 2 and chapter 4.

The philosophical and contemporary view of Hans-Georg Gadamer concerning textual interpretation was then outlined and its implications for biblical understanding examined. The possible compatibility of this theory was identified, providing that the essential ingredients (that is, the "encounter" motif; the prejudicial approach and the "horizon" of question; and an integrative historical view) are found to have adequate support within Scripture. Adequate support was demonstrated, and part I concluded with the observation that Gadamer's hermeneutic was a useful one for ascertaining biblical authority and interpretation.

The study concerning biblical authority turned at this point to explore and examine the additional concern of this book, children and Christian education. With the incontestable linkage between biblical teaching and biblical authority and the pursuit of an authentic biblical model for the education of children, it was deemed necessary to gain comprehensive knowledge of a classic in the field of child development (Jean Piaget) to critically examine his work, and to explore the implications of Piagetian theory for Christian education. Because recognized contributors to the contemporary field of Christian education required consideration, the work of Thomas H. Groome and James Fowler, two primary theorists, was explored. This was the content of part II.

Part III provides a synthesis. First, the claims concerning biblical authority derived from part I will be identified, and a statement concerning criteria for biblical authority proffered. This, in part, responds to the initial question of the thesis, By what criterion or criteria can Christians claim authoritative uniqueness for the Bible?

Second, the rationale for an alternative model will be provided, followed by a statement supporting the use of the Bible with children. The book concludes with a detailed proposal of the "encounter" model as an authentic model in biblical education with children.

Claims Concerning Biblical Authority

The study of biblical authority and interpretation as portrayed in The United Church of Canada, the historical position of Johann August Ernesti, and the contemporary philosophical view of Hans-Georg Gadamer has produced substantive claims. Evidence for these claims has already been demonstrated in the various chapters. For the purpose of clarity, these claims are described in point form.

1. Neither the ultimate authority model, the Christocentric model, nor the contextual model provides a satisfactory approach to Scripture in light of historical, literary, textual and canonical criticism, and theological understanding. This was demonstrated in critical examination of these models in chapter 2.
2. Verbal inspiration, inerrancy, and eternal revelations are invalid criteria with which to defend the authority of Scripture. This is derived from chapter 2 and the examination of Ernesti's biblical hermeneutic.
3. The relationship between Scripture and community is an essential and crucial key. The analysis of Scripture in The United Church of Canada and the exploration of implications for biblical understanding in

Gadamer's hermeneutic highlights this claim for understanding canonical authority.

4. Inspiration or the imagery of "word of God" cannot be limited to canonical scriptures, nor can canonical scriptures possess exclusive monopoly on these concepts. The Bible as canon became the "church's book" during a particular period in its development. (If this were a true axiom for the early Church, that book would have been the Hebrew scriptures, encompassing more material than is contained at the present time in the Old Testament.) That is, at given points in its history, the church, as expressed by leaders in positions of authority, ascertained through various criteria considered appropriate to its *sitz im leben* those works deemed instructional, edifying, doctrinal, etc., for its use. Others within a different context would have chosen differently. In this sense, selection in canonization was arbitrary and, therefore, provides no valid rationale for a closed canon. As Robert W. Funk declares:

The biblical text is made up of human words—Hebrew, Aramaic, and Greek. It is therefore preposterous that the biblical text should be confused with word from God. Nevertheless, it should be recalled that there lurks in the American tradition, as a legacy of Protestant scholasticism, the notion that the biblical text, literally, is word from God. As a consequence of this tradition, man's word about God—what the biblical writers say about God—has come to be understood as God's word to man.[1]

A church proclaiming a theology of a God who speaks through past and present, through established and rebellious orders, through its confessors, skeptics, and threats to faith identity, to be congruent, must expand its canonical covers to include writings previously included, sacred literature since canonization (including contemporary writings) and a critical assessment of those works presently included with a view to exclusion. For as Gadamer affirms: "Even the most genuine and solid tradition . . . needs to be affirmed, embraced, cultivated . . . preservation is as much a freely-chosen action as revolution and renewal."[2] Again, this finding is a result of examining the compatibility of Gadamer's hermeneutic and biblical understanding.

5. The Bible as a "fixed" text does not impede or stifle formation of new theologies. For example, Scripture contains no record of Jesus referring to God as mother and the probability of this having happened is minimal considering the patriarchal culture of his time. We cannot, therefore, determine that it is inappropriate to conceive of God in a feminine as well as masculine disclosure model, for the written word is not the ultimate authority for theological understanding.[3] With ultimate authority disclaimed and historical and progressive revelation upheld, this claim is a logical conclusion.

Criteria for Biblical Authority

The central concern of this book has been the question, By what criterion or criteria can Christians claim authoritative uniqueness for the Bible? Conventional wisdom accepted that biblical authority was lodged in the concepts of verbal inspiration, inerrancy, and eternal revelations, and the inadequacies of these claims have been demonstrated in this text. A positive statement on the source or sources of biblical authority is now demanded.

The Bible is primarily a record of an ancient people's understanding of God (in the Judaeo-Christian tradition) as they attempted to derive meaning from and posit meaning to the historical events in their lives. Authority can be ascribed to the Bible around three foci:

- Community-Authority. This is the authority granted to Scripture by a particular community of faith and supported by its followers. This authority can be graphically named as one's "aura of interest" and relates to prejudicial concerns (as understood by Gadamer) or pre-judgments that necessitate declaration and evaluation for credible interpretation. One presupposition requiring reassessment is the Christian community's approach to the Old Testament, generally viewed in a Christocentric mode. As Gabriel Moran attests: "The Christian has to start taking the Hebrew Bible on its own terms . . . . The child's study of the New Testament, doctrine and church history would be different—and richer—if Judaism were respected as an autonomous way in God's providence."[4]

- Meaning-authority. It is characteristic of human nature to bestow authority upon any work (or person) from which meaning is derived, affecting one's worldview and journey. In relation to Scripture this authority is often connected with community-authority but can also be separate from it. An analogy might be absorption in a theatrical performance to the extent that one's life is changed as a result of meaning derived from it.

- Legacy-authority. Authority is also granted to works (or persons) contributing to the formation of humanity, values, and societal foundations. Again, this relates to community-authority, as persons of this "aura of interest" view themselves as part of the biblical story. It is also separate from it, for the Judaeo-Christian heritage informed by the bible has addressed the whole of humanity, thus, contributing to the human story.

The claim for biblical authority, then, is not as an innate ingredient of the text; authority is an external characteristic granted to it by specific persons or groups of persons in support of core convictions.

An Alternative Model

The encounter model demonstrates and supports an authentic approach to Scripture congruent with philosophical, biblical, and theological understanding. In this model, authority primarily resides in the medium (meaning-authority); that is, the *kerygma* is ascertained through the continuous and integral process of question and response, response and question, as interpreter and text are encountered by each other. The text is approached as response to a question. Thus, the first question of the interpreter is, What is the question to which the text responds? Meaning occurs within the sphere of fusion as illustrated.

There are no indubitable infinite conclusions. Rather, meanings are identified within the historicity of the person and community, that is, historical revelation. The "theology of question" becomes the initial and primary focus. The Book of Job serves as an illustrative example. As identified earlier, in one vignette of the narrative, Yahweh challenges Job with the knowledge that the Divine also has questions requiring Job's response. The Divine does not "answer"; the Divine deepens the question. "Theology of question" claims that the Word addressed to the interpreter is first and foremost in the form of question and any plausible solutions or meanings are followed by subsequent questions.

In the encounter model the interpreter's prejudices are declared, providing the necessary data for criticism together with process and derived conclusions. Identified questions demand critique using as canon the horizon of the text; that is, ascertaining whether the text authenticates the question.

In contrast with Ernesti's hermeneutic (where one meaning resulted from the interpreter addressing the text, implementing an objective, scientific procedure) the encounter model manifests a "spiral of understanding" process (see illustration 6), plunging the interpreter deeper into the text until meaning occurs through the fusion of horizons.

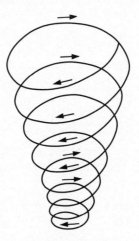

6. Encounter Model

To use a borrowed phrase, the task of the interpreter in relation to the text is to take "citizenship of the place," to identify with the customs, thoughts, and feelings of the text, and to "absorb the atmosphere" of the text.[5]

Children and the Bible

An unattended question remains: Is the Bible an appropriate text for children? One immediate caution in response is the knowledge that the Bible is a text written by adults for adults, though the Bible contains many admonitions and exhortations for the participation of children in its determined truths (examples: Deuteronomy 6:6–7,20; Psalm 78:4). However, it could also be argued that science is equally an adult concept for an adult world. Yet, children are exposed to and often excited by the rudiments of science, which might be considered foreign to their animistic concrete worldview. While the appropriateness of the Bible for children might be argued, the problem is the inadequate biblical resources presently available for children. Most children's books of this nature result in atrophied biblical knowledge or create a necessity for contradictory learnings in later years.

As with the praxis model, children at 7 years of age are certainly apt candidates for the encounter model. Indeed, children aged 5 or 6 can participate in this model in a limited form. For example, in the film *Maybe Yes, Maybe No*,[6] an actual filming of a kindergarten church school class, a five-year-old boy, after two sessions on the story of Noah, queries, "But is it really true?" That inquiry can be classified as a critical examination of the text. The playful nature of the encounter model is also most appropriate for children and for the childhood aspect of all persons.

As with adults, identifying appropriate questions is critical. With children especially, writers and educators are disposed to manipulating biblical texts toward whatever desirable quality or trait is coveted for children to value. For example, sharing is an imperative value for children to apprehend as members of, and contributors to, society. In the eagerness to Christianize the value, the story of the five barley loaves and two fishes (John 6:1–13; Mark 6:34–44) is readily utilized to encapsulate the learning without wrestling with the credibility of this presupposed meaning. An initial perusal of the text suggests that the early Christian writers/editors were attempting to state a conviction about the nature of Jesus as the Christ.

What is required in using the Bible with children is to select texts chosen because the questions to which they respond or the imagery invoked are questions and representations with which children can identify. The psalms are often neglected in teaching children; yet they are rich in symbolism and metaphor and can evoke powerful responses when set in many of the psalm's original context of dance, music, and processional. Psalm 100 is illustrative of this context. Likewise, the parables of Jesus minus moralistic appendages convey poignant and vivid messages. Many of the biblical texts affiliated with the seasons of the church year (Advent, Christmas, Epiphany, Lent, Easter, Pentecost) also provide a base for use with children, for the question is often induced by the occasion and symbolic expressions of it. It is difficult, however, to envisage being inundated with questions from children denotive of Ephesians or First and Second Timothy. What is required is sensitivity to children and respect for the text.

Adults reflecting on their childhood often identify biblical stories as material to be "unlearned" as they matured, discovering that the literal moralistic or conservative interpretations taught during the formative years are unintelligible to their adult world. This is both an unnecessary and inappropriate use of Scripture. Children can encounter Scripture in such a mode that future years can amplify previous learnings as former meanings are revised or discarded in deference to the new. The encounter model sustains this approach to learning.

A Proposal: The Encounter Model

No claim is made in this book for a *sola scriptura* approach in Christian religious education. What it espouses is an authentic or appropriate biblical model when the choice is Scripture. That model has been identified and described as the encounter model. This section considers the relations between three components of the proposed action: children, Scripture, and Christian education, as discussed in chapter 6. This section also outlines an integrated model for The United Church of Canada and other denominations committed to a kindred biblical and educational stance.

Presuppositions (Prejudices, Pre-judgments)

1. The Bible contributes to Christian-identity, who they are as part of the people of God (legacy-authority).
2. The Bible is primarily a "question" rather than "answer" book.
3. The Bible contains diverse understandings of God, situations, and human responses because of various traditions, historicities, and audiences.
4. The Bible may contribute to contemporary decisionmaking through appropriate questions posited to it.
5. Application is an integral part of interpretation, not a separate question after it.

6. Meaning is the moment of truth or understanding occurring during the "fusion of horizon" of text and interpreter and may be synonymous with "word of God," "spirit," "inspiration."
7. Other noncanonical texts and works of art may contain similar prejudices to the above, noting that the Bible is an ancient classic of the Judaeo-Christian heritage and, as such, merits a distinctive place.
8. The church is challenged by its own theology to pursue a critique, assessment, and revision of present canon.
9. All prejudices need to be freely shared for understanding and critique.

Contextual Setting

An integrated model of education and worship with children and adults in intergenerational settings.
- who view the Bible as part of their own history and identity;
- who are motivated to continuous study of it:
- who are committed to the "theology of question";
- who appreciate children in terms of their development;
- who are aware of their own convictions and doubts;
- who are receptive to "moments of truth" in children and adults;
- who are committed to noncognitive and cognitive modes of learning and worship.

Leader of Leaders

- who possesses extensive background in biblical understanding and child development;
- who is committed to extended preparation time regarding content and process.

Format

Leader Preparation

- two evenings per month in community with other leaders for biblical and session preparation.

Learning Sessions

- Sunday, 9:30–10:30 A.M.
- Learning groups for children and adults. Choice given for intergenerational or peer groupings.
- 10:30–11:00 A.M., refreshment break.

Worship

- 11:00–12:00 A.M., following the same theme. (All interested persons are invited. Children without parental interest would be welcomed with the awareness that possibly less effective learning is occurring, especially in the younger years.)

Content: A Sample Session

The initial educational event would require a minimum of two evenings.

I. Leader Preparation
   A. *Getting acquainted and introduction to the program and biblical model*
- not a "forcing" of community but, in an informal way, providing opportunity for ongoing community building;
- briefly sharing format and model;
- questions and response. Participants share their interest in and commitment to the process.

B. *Identifying with the biblical model*
- A sharing of experiences with the Bible.
  Some possibilities:
  My favorite or least favorite Bible story as a child.
  My favorite or least favorite Bible story as an adult.
  Open-ended sentences:
  When I hear the Bible read I think/feel...................... .
  When I read the Bible I think/feel ....
  When I study the Bible I think/feel........................... .
  One question I have concerning the Bible is ....

C. *Participating in the encounter model*
- Choose a text (book, chapter, or set of verses).
- Present through lecture, discussion, research, drama, etc. "What is the question to which this text responds?" (For example, tell the first creation story, Genesis 1:1–2:4, as a possible response to a child's question of the time. "Why can't we play on the Sabbath?" noting in particular 2:3, "God blessed the seventh day and made it holy, because on that day he ceased from all the work he had set himself to do.")
- Invite response. Query—What further questions does this question and response evoke? (Here the presenter acts as an "agent provocateur" or "devil's advocate" to elicit as much questioning and response as possible. Include questions of chapter 5; challenge inappropriate questions).
- Using concordances, commentaries, dictionaries of the Bible, etc., divide into work groups for further research according to questions raised.
- Report back to total group with opportunity for questions and critical commentary by group members.
- Summary provided by presenter, noting possible meanings indicated and further questions.

D. How people learn

Input on child development, adult development, faith development, approaches to learning, etc. (chapters 5 and 6). (Available films: *what do you think?*[7] focusing on the physical, moral, and religious development of children, based on Piagetian theory; *Starting With Nina,*[8] highlighting that critical consciousness is awakened when content of learning is the life-experiences of participants.

Response—Future sessions might include children, inviting response to their likes/dislikes about church, church school, and their questions about life, God, church, etc. (Note: For this process, careful attention must be given to methodology, conducive to the age of the children.

E. Examining format and planning for learning groups and worship

- provide an opportunity for leaders to voice their questions/concerns about format, share in decisionmaking about their own learning group and planning for worship.
- Input on planning session.

F. Closure

- Some brief activity to express the focus of the evening in the spirit of worship.
  Suggestions:
- Have large sheets of blank paper covering a wall with paints and brushes available. Read the first creation story, inviting members, as they desire, to express the reading through paint.
- Read Psalm 8 in unison.
- Sing.

- Read creation story from another culture (native American, Greek mythology, etc.)

II. Learning Groups (1 hour)
A. Getting acquainted
- This provides leaders with opportunity for getting to know participants through greeting them personally and enabling them to get to know one another through group activity. This is also the time to be sensitive to pastoral concerns requiring follow-up (for example: telephone call, visit, etc.).

B. Participating in the encounter model
- An exercise to help participants identify with the text (see examples from leader preparation).
- Recreate the context of the text in a visual way contributive to the stages of development of participants.
- Identify the literary nature of the text (myth, legend, poetry, historical narrative).
- Present the text as response to a particular question through story, drama, music, etc.
- Explore the text with participants through questions elicited from participants.
- Critically examine the meaning(s) of the text through debate, case study, games, consensus, vote, etc.
- Creatively express the meaning(s) of the text through drama, mime, poetry, photography, art, etc.
- Identify questions for further study.

C. Closure
Some brief activity to capture the focus of the session.

D. Refreshment break

Worship (1 bour)

- A planning group or steering committee, consisting of children, adults, and minister(s), meets prior to Sunday to design the worship service compatible with the ages of the participants. Leadership during worship could be provided by children and adults.
- Worship could be designed following the accustomed order, using various methods. Visual imagery, symbols, etc. are important ingredients.
- In addition to Scripture that could be told or read dramatically, mimed, danced, dramatized etc., it would be appropriate to include noncanonical readings. Rather than listening *to* the Word of God, participants might be invited to listen *for* the Word of God or a word *from* God.

Essential to the above outlines are eight major ingredients, congruent with the nature of Church, children, education, and Scripture. These ingredients consist of the following.

- an informal, relaxing environment conducive to learning
- an opportunity for sharing personal thoughts and feelings that necessitate follow-up where called for by the situation
- selected texts related to the questions/concerns of participants
- encountering the text through appropriate questions of leader and participants
- critical examination of the text through questions of leader and participants
- expressing the meaning(s) of the text through creative expression
- identifying unresolved and further questions (articu-

lated and observed) that become the basis for future
planning
- worship designed to be inclusive of children and
adults to enhance the learning theme

The purpose of illustrating this outline is to demonstrate how the encounter model of Scripture might manifest itself in practice. It is not intended to be a treatise on
strategies for implementation or educational methodology and process. Other resources address some of these
concerns, and it is hoped that motivated readers would
pursue the practical implication of the encounter model
for congregational life.

Conclusion

Some books begin with a thesis, and the work that follows provides evidence to support the thesis. This book
began with questions. The primary one, previously identified, concerned biblical authority: By what criterion or
criteria can Christians claim authoritative uniqueness for
the Bible? Another concerned children and biblical education: Is there an acceptable biblical model of education
for children? There were no precluded responses to these
questions; there were conjectures, however. It was sur-
mised that the response to the initial question concerning biblical authority would find its ally with the
contextual model. Instead, it was discovered that the
most adequate response lay in the formulation of an alternative model. Because of this interrogational approach,
the discovery within The United Church of Canada of diverse operative models traceable to its founding denominations was novel. For similar reasons and because of
unfamiliarity with Ernesti's works prior to research, the
limitations of his biblical hermeneutic were unpredict-

able. Prior knowledge of Gadamer indicated that supportive material would emerge.

Another supposition was the improbability of ascertaining a satisfactory biblical educational model for children. In light of research undertaken, an acceptable model was disclosed. Here Piaget was the crucial resource, both in his comprehensive treatise on child development and in identifying the limitations of this work.

The curriculum proposal, therefore, is a practical expression of theoretical research and findings concerning scriptural authority and child development with its identifiable implications for Christian education. For example, the need for adult education, a community context for learning and worshiping, and critical reflection are cited in chapter 6 as a result of examining implications for Christian education in light of Piagetian theory. Claims for biblical authority and resultant criteria concerning that authority are highlighted at the beginning of this chapter. Synthesis occurred in integrating these separate parts into a holistic model of biblical education appropriate with children.

What this book propounds, then, is an authentic model congruent with the authority of Scripture; a critical biblical and theological stance; child development and educational theory. It is an appeal for a marriage between biblical scholarship and church in its educational life with children.

APPENDIX: THEOLOGICAL AND EDUCATIONAL STANCE FOR MINISTRY WITH CHILDREN WORKING UNIT

Preamble

The Ministry with Children Working Unit refers to the biblical images of the body of Christ and of Shalom when it develops policies and programs with, by and for children. These images indicate to us tell us how to live in God's kingdom.

We believe that children are part of the body of Christ—a community in relationship with God through the gift of Jesus Christ, a community in which all members are valued and contribute to the whole. Through baptism, children are recognized as members of the body of Christ, of the people of God, of the Christian church.

Shalom means a unity among people that transcends differences without denying them; a unity in which there is a peace with justice and an interdependence of people, God and the world.

These images affect our understanding of children, their place in congregations, and the purpose of programs they are involved in.

Children and Their Place in the Church

The Ministry with Children working Unit believes that:

- Children, youth and adults are made in God's image.

They are equally valued members of the people of God.

- All people, including children, have equal access to God's love, power, mercy and freedom.
- Children are a means of grace to the community of faith. Jesus tells us that if we welcome children we receive him and the one who sent him. He says that if we want to learn how to receive the kingdom (with confident faith, and with empty hands) and how to become God's representatives in the world (with humility and willingness to serve) we must learn it from the child in our midst.
- Children can teach people of other ages, share in ministry and help others experience God.
- Children are spiritual beings with a sense of the sacred and a relationship with the Divine. Children also have unique physical, emotional, social and intellectual needs at various ages and stages. All of these needs must be taken seriously in worship, education, pastoral care and social action.
- Children do not usually learn or remember the Christian story as a chronological sequence of events. They do learn through meaningful encounters with stories, people and teachings of the faith.
- Children as well as youth and adults, can refuse to respond and to understand God's message. They can participate in and contribute to demonic structures in society. God gives them the freedom to do so.

Purpose of Children's Programs

In programs of worship, social action, Christian Education and nurture, this Unit believes the task is for adults and children together to:

- Relate their lives and their world to God and to Jesus Christ and to all the resources of the Christian faith so that they can live life to its fullest now;
- Share in story and experience the gift of God's kingdom so that they might respond as individuals and as a people by acting in ways that demonstrate love, justice, mercy, peace and equality;
- Address their questions about life today and prepare for a future that will be beyond present experience;
- Accept Jesus Christ as their Keeper and Hope, their Liberator and Friend and be open to the urgings of the Holy Spirit and of God's word.

Our Faith

What is happening in the world affects what we lift up as central aspects of the faith for these times. Therefore, it is important to reflect on the Christian faith and the world as this unit decides what to emphasize in programs involving children, acknowledging that the focus will change in new times and situations.

JESUS CHRIST is the person through whom Christians believe they receive salvation—are made whole—at one with God. Jesus is fully human and fully divine.

We believe that God, through Jesus Christ, proclaimed the good news. As individuals and as a people, we are accepted with all our sins and shortcomings, and are offered the gift of forgiveness.

Jesus is our example for teaching and living the faith. He demonstrates to humanity that God is with us in all of life in the most joyful and in the most hopeless of situations—even death. He showed that new life comes after the pain of dying (even physical dying) to the old way of living.

Jesus declared that God's kingdom of love and justice is

here now, yet still to come. We are still waiting in a situation of suffering and incompleteness.

Through Christ's life, death and resurrection, distinction of age, race, status and sex are transcended so that there is no difference between 'Jews and Gentiles, between slaves and free, between men and women for all are one in Jesus Christ". (Galations 3:28)

GOD is beyond our comprehension. We look to insights concerning God through scripture, Jesus Christ, personal and community experience, recognizing that our comprehension will always be incomplete.

God is ever present, always creating newness in us and in our world and offering to all people freedom, peace and wholeness. God is the creator of the universe, of all people and the giver of all good things. God shares with us the responsibility to care for one another and for God's world.

God is God of love who expects us to seek justice for all people. We are called to respond to God's love and mercy by loving God and all people.

We experience the joy and peace of God through the HOLY SPIRIT.

The Holy Spirit gives us the courage to examine the conflicts in our personal lives and in our world between God's intentions and our actions. The Holy Spirit helps us to trust that God is in the centre of our conflicts, supporting our search for wholeness within us and within the systems of the church and the world.

The Holy Spirit calls all of us not merely to cope with change or to change personally but to be change agents in our world.

Children's Experiences of the World

Children experience many positive things in their lives and the world—the wonder and beauty of nature and the universe—the fun of play, the joy of family friendships—

the warmth of love given and received. But they are also exposed to many negative and ambiguous situations.

- Children can no longer take for granted that being Canadian and being Christian go together; indeed, Christians may be in the minority. They meet people with different religious beliefs as well as people who choose not to believe. They may be exposed to the temptation of setting one group of people or one particular religion over against others.
- They are aware of the unhappiness and the poverty in our own country and the world. They may observe society's willingness to be charitable to those who have less as long as we don't have to change, and our tendency to look after ourselves when the status quo is threatened.
- They sense and share our anxiety about the future. Will our families stay together? Will parents keep their jobs? Will there be jobs for the children of today? Where will the next outbreak of violence be—at home, at school, in the world? Will there be a nuclear war? Will our environment sustain life? What is right and what is wrong?
- They experience a sense of powerlessness and hopelessness along with others in the face of the complexities and difficulties of our world today. They observe in some people a willingness to hand power over to others rather than share in the responsibility of solving the problems of the world.

Concepts to Emphasize Programs Involving Children

Given this context, the Ministry with Children Working Unit believes that programs involving children need to emphasize the following:

GOD LOVES AND CARES FOR EVERYONE AND ALL OF GOD'S CREATION. What affects one person or part of creation, affects all.

To understand and live this concept, children and adults together need to:

- Learn about God's love for the whole world and all the people in it. The highest expression of God's love is found in Jesus, whose life, death and resurrection calls us to seek justice for our world and resist prejudice and hate.
- Convey in appropriate forms that we respect other people's sacred literature and leaders so that we can respect others as people of faith.

WE ARE PART OF A PEOPLE OF FAITH—A BELIEVING, TRUSTING, ACTING PEOPLE.

A Believing People:

As members of the entire human family, the Judaeo-Christian community, the United Church community and a local congregation, we acknowledge there are times when we feel bereft and hopeless. As Christians, we believe we have a faith/story which offers us a sense of belonging, hope and a base from which to live in our world.

To understand and live this concept, children and adults together need to:

- Tell each other the biblical story of the people of God and stories of our Christian tradition, our denominational heritage, and our congregational history;
- Learn the basic doctrines of our faith;
- Discover the context in which the Bible was written and relate it to individual and corporate life today;
- Participate in the symbols and rituals of the Christian Year, such as Advent, Christmas, Epiphany, Lent, Easter, Pentecost.

A Trusting People:

WE CAN TRUST THAT GOD IS WITH US AS WE DEAL WITH LIFE TODAY. As we carry the affirmations of the biblical and traditional story into the uncertainties of the present, we take the risk that Jesus and the prophets called for—to die to the old ways of living and begin a new way of life where all people have access to God's goodness.

To understand and live this concept, adults and children together need to:

- Support one another in their struggles with God—questioning, hating, loving, accepting, forgiving;
- Offer to each other the assurance that God is always faithful;
- Be in relationships with people and the community of faith that lead us to trust God enough that we can confess our wrongdoing and accept God's forgiveness;
- Be open to the Holy Spirit and the possibility of being transformed by experiencing God through Jesus Christ;
- Participate in the sacraments of baptism and communion;
- Share the stories of our personal faith—the joys and the sorrows, the questions and concerns we have about our faith, our lives and the world;
- Take time together and alone to pray and open ourselves to God, to a new understanding of God and to the new directions in which God may be moving us;

An Acting People:

WE ARE CALLED TO ACT SO THAT GOD'S LOVE CAN BE SHARED WITH THE WORLD THROUGH US; SO THAT WE AND THE WORLD CAN LIVE AS GOD INTENDED.

To understand and live this concept, adults and children together need to:

- Share the biblical story of God's desire to bring hope and wholeness to individuals and to restore peace and justice to the world;
- Experience situations in which there is poverty, loneliness, injustice. Analyze these experiences to understand the role of people and systems in them and to offer the hope that evil can be overcome.
- Identify our feelings of hurt and oppression and relate them to the poor, sick, suffering, imprisoned so that we can understand them as people with worth and dignity, not as objects of pity or charity;
- Use our gifts to serve and care for the lonely, the wounded, the needy, sick, imprisoned— aware of the value of the gifts that we receive from those we seek to serve;
- Receive ministry and care from other people;
- Undertake projects that help bring about justice and peace in our world;
- Give leadership in worship, education, pastoral care, and social action in our congregations.

Style of Implementation of These Concepts

The Ministry with Children Working Unit feels that these concepts need to be presented in a style that as much as possible:

- Integrates worship, learning, caring and action— children, youth and adults—body, mind and spirit;
- Consults with children to discover their interests, questions and concerns about the content and process of education, pastoral care, worship and action;

- Provides experiences and activities—that respect differences in interests and abilities at various ages and stages—that uses resources besides books: people, community, the world, paints, clay, music, drama, meditation, film, etc.

Notes

Introduction

1. Edgar Krentz, *The Historical-Critical Method* (Philadelphia: Fortress Press, 1975), p. 18.
2. Ibid., p. 19.
3. F. L. Cross, ed., *The Oxford Dictionary of the Christian Church,* 2d ed., revised by F. L. Cross and E. A. Livingstone (Oxford: Oxford University Press, 1974), p. 468.

Chapter 1. Three Models of Biblical Authority

1. "Basis of Union" in *The Manual: The United Church of Canada,* 24th rev. ed. 1983 (Toronto: United Church of Canada, 1928, 1983), p. 11.
2. Ibid.
3. Ibid., p. 12.
4. Ibid., p. 14.
5. "Confessing our Faith" in *24th General Council Record of Proceedings* (Toronto: United Church of Canada, 1982), p. 377.
6. Ibid.
7. Ibid., p. 380.
8. Ibid., p. 378.
9. Ibid.
10. *Statement of Faith: A Statement Prepared by a Commission Authorized by the Seventh General Council and Appointed by the Board of Evangelism and Social Services* (Toronto: United Church of Canada, 1940), pp. 5, 6.
11. *A Catechism: An Expression of Faith* (Toronto: United Church of Canada, 1944), pp. 6, 12.
12. While none of the founding churches illustrate these models in their entirety, it is observed that all three founding denominations have a proclivity for the particular model identified. It is also interesting to note that the former moderator of the United Church, Dr. Clarke MacDonald, who highlighted the Christocen-

tric model, is of Methodist background.

13. *The Confession of Faith;* Agreed upon by The Assembly of Divines at Westminster: Examined and approved, Anno 1647, by The General Assembly of The Church of Scotland: and ratified by Acts of Parliament 1649 and 1690. Printed by order of the Synod of The Presbyterian Church of Canada in connection with the Church of Scotland, For the use of The Church in Canada (Toronto: James and Thomas A. Starke, 1834), pp. 7, 8.
14. Ibid.
15. William Gregg, *History of the Presbyterian Church in the Dominion of Canada* (Toronto: Toronto Presbyterian and Publishing House, 1885), pp. 19, 24.
16. *The Acts and Proceedings of the 49th General Assembly of The Presbyterian Church in Canada: Port Arthur, Ontario, June 6– 14, 1923* (Canada: Murray Printing Co., 1923), p. 85.
17. Ibid., p. 12.
18. R. W. Dale, *Manual of Congregational Principles* (Great Britain: Hodder and Stroughton, 1884), p. 38.
19. Ibid., pp. 36–40.
20. William E. Barton, *The Law of Congregational Usage* (USA: Advance Publishing Co., 1916), p. 10.
21. William E. Barton, *Congregational Manual and Rules of Order* (n.p., n.d.), p. 227.
22. Wilson R. Buxton, *A Manual For Christian Instruction* (New York: Pilgrim Press, 1903), pp. 5–9.
23. "Compendium of Forms" in Barton, *Congregational Manual and Rules of Order,* p. 231.
24. *The Discipline, 1922: The Doctrine and Discipline of the Methodist Church in Canada, 1922* (Toronto: Methodist Book and Publishing House, 1923), p. 13.
25. Ibid.
26. Ibid., p. 347.
27. Ibid., p. 373.
28. Colin W. Williams, *John Wesley's Theology Today* (Nashville: Abingdon Press, 1960), p. 26.
29. *Acts and Proceedings . . . Presbyterian Church,* 1923, p. 85.
30. Claris Edwin Silcox, *Church Union in Canada: Its Causes and Consequences* (Institute of Social and Religious Research, n.d.), pp. 133, 134.
31. Ibid., p. 127.

Chapter 2. Biblical Authority and Curricula

1. "Theological and Educational Stance" for Ministry with Children Working Unit, the United Church of Canada, 1982, p. 2.

2. Ibid., p. 4.
3. Ibid.
4. Ibid., p. 4.
5. Ibid., pp. 1–2.
6. Ibid., p. 4.
7. Ibid.
8. Ibid., p. 4.
9. Ibid., p. 6.
10. Ibid., p. 5.
11. *Prospectus: The New Curriculum* (Toronto: United Church of Canada, 1961), p. 8.
12. Ibid., p. 12.
13. Ibid., p. 21.
14. Ibid.
15. Ibid., pp. 221–22.
16. Ibid., p. 22.
17. Ibid., p. 33.
18. Donald M. Mathers, *The Word and the Way* (Toronto: United Church Publishing House, 1962), p. 95.
19. Ibid., p. 99.
20. Ibid., pp. 100-101.
21. *Junior Teacher's Guide—Year 1* (Toronto: United Church Publishing House, 1964), pp. 1, 3.
22. Ibid., p. 3.
23. Ibid.
24. *Doing Church Education Together: Why and How JED Works* (Joint Educational Development, 1978), p. 6.
25. Ibid., p. 6.
26. Ibid., p. 8.
27. Ibid., p. 13.
28. Carol Wehrheim, ed., *Guide to Curriculum Choice* (Elgin, IL: Brethren Press, 1981), p. 36.
29. Ibid., p. 37.
30. Robert E. Koenig, *Christian Education: Shared Approaches; An Overview* (United Church Press, 1975), p. 13.
31. *Children's Bible Series; Junior Teacher's Resource Guide: Knowing the Bible Story; March–May, 1984* (Crawfordsville, IN: Geneva Press, 1983), p. 17.
32. Ibid., p. 40.
33. Ibid., p. 41.
34. Ibid., p. 62.
35. *Children's Bible Series; Junior Teacher's Resource Guide: Knowing the Bible Story; September–November, 1983* (Crawfordsville, IN: Geneva Press, 1983), p. 11.
36. Ibid.
37. Wehrheim, *Guide to Curriculum Choice,* p. 41.

38. Ibid., p. 90.
39. *Joy Director's Manual* (Minneapolis: Winston Press, n.d.), pp. 4–11.
40. *Joy 3: A Religious Education Program for Grade Three Teacher Manual* (Minneapolis: Winston Press, 1976), pp. 36–44.
41. *Joy 1: A Religious Education Program for Grade One Teacher Manual* (Minneapolis: Winston Press, 1976), p. 7.
42. *Joy 3,* p. 7.
43. Wehrheim, *Guide to Curriculum Choice,* p. 91.
44. "Read Me First" in *Loaves and Fishes,* vol. 6, Spring (Toronto: United Church of Canada, 1984), p. 7.
45. "A Whale of a Tale" in *Loaves and Fishes,* vol. 6, Spring, p. 2.
46. "Blessed Are the Peacemakers" in *Loaves and Fishes,* vol. 6, Spring, pp. 2–3.
47. Ibid., p. 8.
48. Paul J. Achtemeier, *The Inspiration of Scripture: Problems and Proposals* (Philadelphia: Westminster Press, 1980), p. 59.
49. Ibid., pp. 160–61.
50. Frederick E. Greenspahn, ed., *Scripture in the Jewish and Christian Traditions: Authority, Interpretation, Relevance* (Nashville: Abingdon Press, 1982), p. 211.
51. Ibid., p. 205.
52. James Sanders, *Torah and Canon* (Philadelphia: Fortress Press, 1972), p. 81.
53. Greenspahn, *Scripture in Jewish and Christian Traditions,* p. 145.
54. Ibid., p. 146.
55. Ibid., p. 213.

Chapter 3. A Classical Protestant Model of Biblical Authority

1. Peter Gay, *The Enlightenment: An Interpretation; The Rise of Modern Paganism* (New York, Alfred A. Knopf, 1967), p. 3.
2. Ibid.
3. Edgar Krentz, *The Historical-Critical Method, pp. 9– 10.*
4. John Edwin Sandys, *A History of Classical Scholarship* vol. III; *The 18th Century in Germany and the 19th Century in Europe and the USA* (New York: Hafner Publishing Co., 1967), p. 11.
5. Ibid., p. 12.
6. Ibid., p. 13.
7. Cross, *Oxford Dictionary,* p. 468.
8. Jaroslav Pelikan, *From Luther to Kierkegaard: A Study in the History of Theology* (St. Louis: Concordia Publishing House, 1950), p. 88.

9. Richard E. Palmer, *Hermeneutics: Interpretation Theory ·in Schleiermacher, Dilthey, Heidegger and Gadamer* (Evanston: Northwestern Press, 1969), p. 82.

10. Ibid., p. 38.

11. Gay, *The Enlightenment,* p. 378.

12. Milton S. Terry, *Biblical Hermeneutics: A treatise on the interpretation of the Old and New Testaments* (Grand Rapids, MI: Zondervan Publishing House, 1974), p. 707.

13. Krentz, *Historical-Critical Method,* p. 18.

14. Hans Frei, *The Eclipse of Biblical Narrative: A Study in Eighteenth and Nineteenth Century Hermeneutics* (New Haven and London: Yale University Press, 1974), p. 251.

15. Moses Stuart, trans., *Principles of Interpretation,* 4th ed., translated from the Latin of J. A. Ernesti (New York: Dayton and Saxton, 1842), p. 27.

16. E. D. Hirsch is a modern exponent of this view, arguing that the only valid interpretation of a text is the author's intended meaning. See E.D. Hirsch, *Validity in Interpretation* (New Haven: Yale University Press, 1953).

17. Stuart, *Principles of Interpretation, p. 17.*

18. Ibid., p. 14.

19. Ibid., p. 100.

20. Ibid., pp. 14-15.

21. Ibid., p. 15.

22. Ibid., p. 17.

23. Ibid., p. 45.

24. Ibid., p. 19.

25. Ibid., p. 21.

26. Ibid., pp. 25–45.

27. Ibid., p. 67.

28. Ibid., p. 26.

29. Ibid., p. 28.

30. Ibid., p. 79.

31. Ibid.

32. Ibid., p. 59.

33. Ibid., p. 60.

34. Ibid., pp. 60–61.

35. Ibid., p. 64.

36. Ibid., p. 79.

37. Ibid., pp. 31–32.

38. Ibid., pp. 76–77.

39. Cross, Oxford Dictionary, p. 468.

40. Ibid., p. 23.

41. Ibid., pp. 31– 32.

42. Pelikan, From Luther to Kierkegaard, p. 83.

43. Ibid.

44. Krentz, *The Historical-Critical Method,* p. 18.
45. Ibid., p. 19.
46. Robert M. Grant, *A Short History of the Interpretation of the Bible,* 2d ed., revised and enlarged by Robert Grant with David Tracy (Philadelphia Press, 1984), p. 127.

Chapter 4. A Textual Model of Biblical Authority

1. J. D. Kaplan, ed., *Dialogues of Plato: Apology, Crito, Phaedo, Symposium, Republic,* trans. Benjamin Jovett (New York: Washington Square Press, 1950), chap. V, pp. 473–75.
2. Hans-Georg Gadamer, *Truth and Method,* translation of *Wahrheit und Methode* by J. C. B. Mohr, Tubingen, 1960 (New York: Crossroad Publishing Co., 1982), p. 358.
3. Ibid., p. 107.
4. Ibid., pp. 275–76.
5. Ibid., pp. xix–xx.
6. Ibid., p. xix.
7. Ibid., p. xxi.
8. Ibid., pp. xxiii, 107, 246.
9. Ibid., pp. 258, 261.
10. Ibid., p. 263.
11. Ibid., p. 401.
12. Ibid.
13. Ibid., p. 404.
14. Ibid., p. 346.
15. Ibid., p. 400.
16. Ibid., p. 350.
17. Ibid., p. 240.
18. Ibid., p. 238.
19. Ibid., pp. 240, 244, 246.
20. Ibid., p. 263.
21. Ibid., 264.
22. Ibid., 266.
23. Ibid., p. 265.
24. Ibid., 249.
25. Ibid., 248.
26. Ibid.
27. Ibid., p. 250.
28. Ibid.
29. Ibid., p. 258.
30. *The Apology,* in Edith Hamilton, ed., *Plato: The Collected Dialogues,* Bollingen Series LXXI (Princeton, NJ: Princeton University Press, 1961), 1 21d, p. 8.

31. Gadamer, *Truth and Method,* p. 327.
32. Ibid., p. 326.
33. Ibid., p. 269.
34. Ibid., p. 327.
35. Ibid., p. 336.
36. Ibid., pp. 333, 337.
37. Ibid., p. 337.
38. Ibid., p. 329.
39. Ibid., pp. 274–75
40. Ibid., pp. 274–75.
41. Ibid., pp. 346–47.
42. Ibid., p. 331.
43. Ibid., p. 340.
44. Ibid., p. 445.
45. Ibid., p. 347.
46. Ibid., p. 349.
47. Palmer, *Hermeneutics,* p. 180.
48. Sanders, *Torah and Canon,* pp. xiv– xv.
49. Elaine Pagels, *The Gnostic Gospels,* Vintage Books edition (New York: Random House, Inc., 1981), pp. xiv–xv.
50. Robert W. Funk, *Parables and Presence* (Philadelphia: Fortress Press, 1982), p. 153.
51. Achtemeier, *Inspiration of Scripture,* p. 119.
52. Jacob Neusner, *Between Time and Eternity: The Essentials of Judaism* (Encino, CA: Dickenson Publishing Co., 1975), p. 80.
53. Ibid., p. 16.
54. Norman Perrin, *Rediscovering The Teachings of Jesus* (New York: Harper & Row, 1976), p. 56.

Chapter 5. Jean Piaget's Developmental Model

1. Rudolf Bultmann, *Kerygma and Myth* by Rudolf Bultmann and five critics, edited by Hans Werner Bartsch (New York: Harper & Row, 1961), p. 1.
2. Jean Piaget, *The Child's Conception of the World,* trans. Joan and Andrew Tomlinson (St. Albans, UK: Granada Publishing Limited, 1973), pp. 45–76.
3. Ibid., pp. 79–101.
4. Ibid., pp. 101–105.
5. Ibid., pp. 110-48.
6. Ibid., pp. 194–219.
7. Ibid., pp. 220-33.
8. Ibid., pp. 242– 43.
9. Ibid., pp. 252–60.

10. Ibid., p. 285.
11. Ibid., p. 294.
12. Ibid., pp. 286–375.
13. Ibid., pp. 375–95.
14. Ibid., pp. 108, 149.
15. Ibid., p. 420.
16. Ibid., p. 152.
17. Ibid., p. 414.
18. Ibid., p. 415.
19. Ibid., pp. 416–17.
20. Ibid., p. 418.
21. Ibid., p. 399.
22. Ibid., p. 400.
23. Ibid., p. 189.
24. Jean Piaget, *The Child and Reality,* trans. Arnold Rosin (New York: Grossman Publishers, 1973), pp. 54–61.
25. Ibid., p. 54.
26. Jean Piaget and Barbel Inhelder, *The Psychology of the Child,* translated from the French by Helen Weaver (New York: Basic Books, 1969), p. 5. Piaget defines assimilation as "that reality data are treated or modified in such a way as to become incorporated into the structure of the subject."
27. Ibid., p. 7.
28. Piaget, *Child and Reality,* p. 54.
29. Herbert Ginsburg and Sylvia Opper, *Piaget's Theory of Intellectual Development: An Introduction* (Englewood Cliffs, NJ: Prentice-Hall, 1969), p. 36.
30. Piaget, *Child and Reality,* p. 54.
31. Ibid.
32. Piaget, *Psychology of the Child,* p. 10.
33. Piaget, *Child and Reality,* p. 55.
34. Ginsburg, *Piaget's Theory of Intellectual Development,* p. 53.
35. Piaget, *Child and Reality,* p. 55.
36. Ibid.
37. Ibid.
38. Piaget, *Psychology of the Child,* p. 12.
39. Ibid.
40. Piaget, *Child and Reality,* p. 57.
41. Ginsburg, *Piaget's Theory of Intellectual Development,* p. 73.
42. Piaget, *Child and Reality,* p. 57.
43. Piaget, *Psychology of the Child,* p. 71.
44. Piaget, *Child and Reality,* p. 58.
45. Piaget, *Psychology of the Child,* p. 99.
46. Ginsburg, *Piaget's Theory of Intellectual Development,* pp. 166–67.

47. Piaget, *Child and Reality,* p. 58.
48. Piaget, *Psychology of βthe Child,* p. 100.
49. Ginsburg, *Piaget's Theory of Intellectual Development,* p. 167.
50. Ibid., p. 165.
51. Piaget, *Child and Reality,* p. 59.
52. Ibid., pp. 59–60 and Piaget, *Psychology of the Child,* pp. 132, 141.
53. Jean Piaget, *The Moral Judgment of the Child* (London: Routledge and Kegan Paul, 1983), p. 1.
54. Ibid., pp. 16– 17.
55. Ibid., p. 18.
56. Ibid., p. 202.
57. Ibid., p. 193.
58. Ibid.
59. Ibid. and Piaget, *Psychology of the Child,* p. 124.
60. Ibid., p. 125.
61. Ibid., p. 126.
62. Piaget, *Moral Judgment of the Child*, p. 194.
63. Ibid.
64. Piaget, *Psychology of the Child,* p. 5.
65. Peter L. Berger, *The Sacred Canopy: Elements of a Sociological Theory of Religion* (New York: Doubleday & Co., 1969), p. 84.
66. Lawrence Kohlberg, "The Cognitive-Developmental Approach to Moral Education" in *Readings in Human Development and Learning* (Dubuque, IA: Kendall/Hunt Pub. Co., 1976), p. 105.
67. Ibid.
68. Donald M. Joy, ed., *Moral Development Foundations: Judeo-Christian Alternatives to Piaget/Kohlbert* (Nashville: Abingdon Press, 1983), p. 30.
69. In the film *What Do You Think?* (USA: Division of Mass Media of the Presbyterian Church, 1975), Dr. David Elkind interviews both girls and boys, basing both his research and interviews on Piaget's theories.
70. Joy, *Moral Development Foundations,* pp. 30–31.
71. Edward Robinson, *The Original Vision: A Study of the Religious Experience of Childhood* (New York: The Seabury Press, 1983), p. 14.
72. Ibid., p. 28.
73. Ibid., p. 32.
74. Ibid., p. 35.
75. Ibid., ix.
76. Ibid., p. 8.
77. Kohlberg, "The Cognitive-Developmental Approach to Moral Education," p. 105.

Chapter 6. Implications for Christian Education

1. Cross, *Oxford Dictionary,* p. 1156.
2. Gabriel Moran, *Religious Education Development: Images for the Future* (Minneapolis: Winston Press, 1983), pp. 137–38.
3. John Dewey, *Experience and Education,* copyright 1938 Kappa Delta Pi (New York: MacMillan Pub. Co., 1963), p. 89.
4. Ibid., p. 46.
5. Thomas H. Groome, *Christian Religious Education* (San Francisco: Harper & Row, 1980), p. 145.
6. Ibid., pp. 139–45, 250.
7. Paulo Freire, *Pedagogy of the Oppressed* (New York: Continuum Publishing Corp., 1981), p. 40.
8. Ibid., p. 59. Friere's concept of the "banking" method is similar to the image of a funnel. The teacher with the knowledge pours it into the ignorant student. In this view, the teachers are the subjects in learning and the students are the objects.
9. Ibid., p. 101.
10. Ibid., p. 75.
11. Ibid., p. 119.
12. Groome, *Christian Religious Education,* p. 176.
13. Ibid., p. 177.
14. Dewey, *Experience and Education,* pp. 22–23.
15. Groome, *Christian Religious Education,* p. 184.
16. Ibid., p. 208.
17. Ibid., pp. 250–51.
18. Ibid., p. 214.
19. Kenneth Stokes, ed., *Faith Development in the Adult Life Cycle* (New York: W. H. Sadlier, 1982), p. 31.
20. Groome, *Christian Religious Education,* pp. 76–77.
21. James Fowler, *Stages of Faith: The Psychology of Human Development and the Quest for Meaning* (San Francisco: Harper & Row, 1981), pp. 121, 133, 149, 172–73, 182, 198–200.
22. Ibid., pp. 146, 161.
23. Ibid., p. 164.

Chapter 7. A New Encounter Model of Biblical Authority

1. Robert W. Funk, *Parables and Presence* (Philadelphia: Fortress Press, 1982), p. 158.
2. Gadamer, *Truth and Method,* p. 25.
3. Moran, *Religious Education Development,* p. 139.
4. Ibid., p. 201.
5. Sibilla Aleramo, *A Woman,* trans. Rosaline Delmar (Berkeley:

University of California Press, 1980), p. 45.
6. Film, *Maybe Yes, Maybe No* (Toronto: PVS Productions, 1978).
7. Film, *What Do You Think?* (Division of Mass Media, Presbyterian Church, 1975).
8. Film, *Starting With Nina* (Toronto: Development Education Centre, 1978).

Appendix

1. Piaget, *Child's Conception of the World,* p. 45.
2. Ibid., p. 14.
3. Ibid., p. 16.
4. Ibid., pp. 17–18.
5. Ibid., p. 18.
6. Ibid., p. 16.
7. Ibid., p. 19.
8. Ibid.
9. Ibid., p. 20.
10. Ibid., pp. 21–22.
11. Ibid., pp. 24, 26.
12. Ibid., p. 21.
13. Ginsburg, *Piaget's Theory of Intellectual Development,* p. 118.

Index

Abortion, 18
Abraham, 33
Achtemeier, Paul J., 38–39, 78
Analogy, grammatical, 53
Animism, 87, 90–92, 101
Artificialism, 90, 91–92, 101
Ast, Friedrich, 49
Athanasius, 78
Augustine, 48, 53
Authority, biblical, xi–xv; *See* Christocentric model, of biblical authority. *See also* Contextual model, of biblical authority; and curricula, 19–45; encounter model for, 125–43; and Ernesti's biblical hermeneutic, 48–59; problem of, and the Protestant church, xiii; textual model of, 61–81; three models of, xiii, 3–18, 37–44, 125. *See also* Ultimate authority model, of biblical authority

Berger, Peter, 102–3
Bible, the 9–10; authority of the. *See* Authority, biblical; and current social issues, 18; diversity of, 40, 42; and the encounter model, 135–38; the encounter motif in, 70–74, 81; as a "faith heritage" resource, 33; great themes of, 29; as a guide for Christian living, 33; harmony and integration in, 38, 40; inerrancy of, 40–41; integrative historical view of, 79–81; interpretation of, xiii; as the object of faith, 39; "prejudicial approach" to, 74–78, 81; as synonymous with the Word of God, 39; truth and meaning in, 42; and revelation, 26, 33. *See also* God, word of
Bultmann, Rudolf, 86

Canaan, conquest of, 73
Canonization, xii, 78, 128–29

Catholicism, Roman, xi
Child development, 20, 33
Children: assumptions about, 109; the Bible as a text for, 132–35; Christian education of. *See* Christian education, of children; moral judgment of, 86, 106; place of, in the church, 145–46; programs for 146–53; religious development of, 92–93, 105–6, 110–22; worldview of, 86–93, 106, 148–49
Children's Bible Series, 27–31, 37
Christ: body of, 21; centrality of, 25, 27; as central to both Testaments, 16–17, 42–43; God's revelation in, 29. *See also* Jesus
Christian education, of children, xiv–xv, 19–20, 146–53; "Knowing the Word" approach to, 29, 30–31; "praxis" model of, 116–18, 133; relevance of Piaget's psychology to, 111–16; "shared-praxis" model of, 118–20. *See also* Curricula
Christianity, orthodox, xii
Christians, early, 43, 44
Christocentric model, of biblical authority, 3–4, 7–11, 16–17, 27, 30; critical examination of, 42–44
Church: meaning and mission of the, 7; union, opposition to, 17–18
Collins, Anthony, 50
Commandments, Ten, 4–5
Community, Christian, 149–50
Congregational church, 10–11, 13–16
Contextual model, of biblical authority, 3–4, 5–7, 11, 13–16, 30; critical examination of, 41–42; preparation time for, 37
Cosmology. *See* Worldview
Curricula: and biblical authority, 19–45; as child-centered, 33; and the integration of theory and practice, 37

of, 87; worldview of, 87. *See also* Christ
Joint Educational Development (JED), 27–28
Jonah, story of, 35
Joy curriculum, 31–34, 37
Judaism, Jesus' critique of, 43–44
Judgment, moral, 86, 104, 106
Junior Teacher's Guide—Year 1, 26–27

Kant, Immanuel, 47, 97
Kohlberg, Lawrence, 103, 104
Knowledge, in Piaget, 110
Krentz, Edgar, xiii, 50, 58

Language: in Gadamer, 63–64, 69–70; inclusive, xv, 18; religious, 113; as a view of the world, 63–64. *See also* Hermeneutics
Lau, Franz, 50
Learning: groups, 139–40; in Piaget, 109–10
Loaves and Fishes, 20, 34–37, 41

Mathers, Donald M., 26
Melanchthon, 52
Methodist Church, 10–11, 16–17
Ministry with Children Working Unit, 19, 21, 34, 37, 145
Modernity: and faith, 25; and tradition, 47
Moral: development, in Piaget, 97–101; judgment, 86, 104, 106
Moran, Gabriel, 113, 130

Nature/Nurture Paradox, 102–3, 106
Neusner, Jacob, 79–80
Nuclear: disarmament, 18; war, threat of, 35, 36

Palmer, R. E., 50
Parks, Rosa, 104
Paul (saint), 22, 39
Perrin, Norman, 80
Piaget, Jean, xiv–xv, 20, 33, 85–122; the child's worldview in, 87–93, 101, 110; cognitive development in, 93–97, 101; developmental model of, 85–107, 109–11; knowledge in, 110; learning in, 109; moral development in, 97–101; the phases of realism in, 92; religious development in, 92–93, 110–11, 112; theories of, implications for Christian education, 109–22, 126
Pietism, xiii
Pluralism, during the Enlightenment, 47
Poverty, issue of, 18, 149
Prayer, 33
Presbyterian church, 10–13
Prospectus, The, 24–26
Protestant church, xi–xii
Psychology, developmental, xiv–xv. *See also* Piaget, Jean

Racism, 40
Raikes, Robert, 111
Rationalism, and orthodoxy, in Ernesti, 49, 50, 55
Reason, as ultimate authority, 47
Redemption, 29
Reformation, Protestant, 47–48
Religion, and children in Piaget, 109, 110–11
Revelation, 26
Robinson, Edward, 105–6, 112
Romanticism, Gadamer's critique of, 66

Sanders, James, 40
Schleiermacher, Friedrich, 49, 57, 62
Schweitzer, Albert, 59
Scripture. *See* Bible, the
Semler, Johan Salomo, 58
Sexism, 40
Shalom, concept of, 21, 35–36, 145
Sin, 29
Socrates, 62, 67
Stendahl, Krister, 40, 43–44
Subjectivity, 59

Terry, Milton, 50
Text: and interpreter, 59, 64, 67–68, 81, 131–32; in Gadamer, 62, 67–70; —s, burial of sacred, 78. *See also* Hermeneutics; Language

Ultimate authority model, of biblical authority, 3–5, 11–13, 37; critical examination of, 38–41